An Illustrated History of
LLANGOLLEN

An Illustrated
History of
LLANGOLLEN

Gordon Sherratt

CEIRIOG PRESS

Published by: The Ceiriog Press, 6 Vicarage Road, Llangollen,
Denbighshire LL20 8HF, Wales, United Kingdom.

www.ceiriogpress.com

British Library Cataloguing in Publication Data.
A catalogue record for this book is available from the British Library.

ISBN 0-9530336-4-3

Designed and typeset by:
Celtic Publishing Services, 6 Vicarage Road, Llangollen,
Denbighshire LL20 8HF.

Printed and bound in Great Britain by: Redwood Books, Trowbridge.

Publisher's Note:
Although every effort has been made to trace and contact copyright
holders before publication, this has not always been possible. If
notified, the publisher will be pleased to rectify any errors or
omissions at the earliest opportunity.
Some of the photographs reproduced in this book are from poor
quality and/or aged originals. The publisher has taken every
opportunity to enhance quality wherever possible, but in some cases
of particularly interesting subject matter, a decision to publish the
photograph regardless of quality has been taken.
Care has also been taken when labelling photographs, but if any
errors have been made please contact the publisher and they will be
rectified at the first available opportunity.

Dedication

This book is dedicated to the good people (past and present) of Llangollen — the town which I am privileged to call home.

Foreword

by The Right Honourable Lady Trevor of Brynkinallt.

Those of us who are fortunate enough to be included in Gordon Sherratt's large circle of friends have always appreciated his vast knowledge of Wales, especially North Wales and the Llangollen area in particular.

As an architectural historian with a working acquaintance of the Welsh language, he was the ideal person to introduce us to this area. His connections with several of the old North Wales families also enable him to include many fascinating anecdotes and early photographs for us to enjoy.

I am confident that this book will give great pleasure to all who read it.

Those familiar with Gordon's earlier book, *A Hurried History of Llangollen,* will enjoy this longer and more detailed volume. Newcomers will find much to delight and amuse whilst learning about this interesting and historic town set in the beautiful valley of the River Dee.

Contents

18th century travellers seeking directions. From an original painting in the author's collection by Thomas Rowlandson (1756–1827).

Introduction

John Ruskin, the great 19th century romantic and man of letters, wrote, "The Dee itself is a quite perfect mountain stream, and the village of Llangollen — one of the most beautiful and delightful in Wales". Today the *Llangollen Official Guide* says much the same in rather more words.

However, it was not always ever thus! Georgian travellers bumping about in uncomfortable carriages were generally of the opinion that it was "A poor town", saving their superlatives to describe the grandeur of the surrounding scenery.

In 1880 the author of *Jones' Picturesque Views* writing from the grandiose address of the 'Temple of the Muses, Finsbury Square', was pleased to offer confirmation:

"Llangollen — this is a small poor looking town, consisting of a few narrow streets, and the houses being built of dark, shaley stone, gives it a dingy and forbidding aspect. But being a thoroughfare on the great Irish Road and situated in an interesting spot, it is enlivened by the daily passing of travellers, and occasionally enriched by an influx of wealthy strangers, who take up their abode here, to visit places in the vicinity, and survey the beauties of its celebrated vale."

Mr. Black, in his *Picturesque Guide* (1870) considered the town to be lively but ...

"The streets are narrow, irregular and ill paved; and the houses are, for the most part, old and mean, but gradually giving place to modern and more handsome dwellings."

So, there was hope. Today's architectural historians may perhaps be a little more divided in their opinion of these 'handsome dwellings'! In 1930 Ward Locks described Llangollen as a clean, if "primitive looking town" and, after a romantically-glowing account of the surrounding scenery, is pleased to record that some of England's more eminent physicians considered Llangollen to be one of the healthiest of inland resorts where octogenarians were not exceptional. Furthermore, "A visit to the old churchyards will show that such was the case long ago — while not a few centenarians have spent their lives in this beautiful valley". This must be a comfort to us all.

In 1898 the travel writer A.G. Bradley records, "finding a few lanes, that is to say, of old cottages, leading inconsequentially upward, but at an angle of forty-five degrees, and to no goal in particular". These he seems to prefer to the modern areas of the town. Earlier, when describing in flattering terms the natural beauty of the Vale, he used the derogatory words "amid which Llangollen lies as something of a desecration!" But by 1929, "the village has this long time ceased to be the unsophisticated Arcady [as described by the Ladies of Llangollen, whose] architectural deficiencies — matter nothing — since it is the situation and surroundings which make it famous".

In truth, the same applies today. Few who are bent upon discovering a town brim-full of architectural delights would see Llangollen as their Mecca. True, there are some gems to be discovered for those with the patience to seek them out, but it is almost *because* of the curious mish-mash of façades and uncomplimentary building styles that the town has developed its peculiar charm.

Both the grandeur and gentle beauty of the surrounding countryside have remained ever with us. One feels it is this, together with the very individual character of what is still after all little more than a village, that has developed the personalities of those who have lived their lives here.

The biased — of whom the writer is one — would say that Llangollen people are special people. Who, we wonder, will disagree?

The river and the bridge have perforce always influenced life in Llangollen. The Dee, like the bridge that spans it, has a very individual character of its own and its influence will never be far away as our history unfolds. This modern aerial photograph shows clearly how the town is divided and dominated.

As we shall read later, before the advent of the railways much of the old town was built around the Green on the northern bank of the river, straggling out along the Trevor Road in the direction of what was to become an area of industrial development.

The Bridge has traditionally been a place for exchanging news and views, particularly during the summer months when the v-shaped packhorse embrasures are ideally suited to leisurely loitering. Much of what is to follow would have been the topic of such conversations in earlier times.

Aerial view of Llangollen showing the importance of the Bridge and how it links the two halves of the town.

Map of Denbighshire dated 1667 on which the township of Pengwern is given equal status to that of Llangollen.

Pre-history

The Llangollen area must have been well-populated in pre-historic times. Apart from the Bronze Age fortifications of Dinas Brân and the Iron Age fort at Penygaer, Cannon Ellis Davies in his *Prehistoric and Roman Remains of Denbighshire* lists no fewer that thirty-two cairns and tumuli. Five of them are on the Berwyn foothills south of the Dee, and twenty-seven are to be found on the Eglwyseg and Trevor Rocks.

Of all the tumuli, one of the most interesting is directly above Dinbren Ucha Farm. It is easily reached by a diagonal footpath up the escarpment and easily found because a wire fence cuts right across its length. In fact, it was when a workman was cutting holes for the posts of this very fence that some of the contents of the tumulus were found. The fragments of clay urn pottery and bones were sent to Mr. Kenrick of Birmingham who, at that time, owned the Dinbren estate. Sir Arthur Keith reported that they were fragments of the cremation of a human body, the unburned shoulder blade of an ox and ribs of sheep.

Further along and walking eastwards there is a perfect stone circle, fifty-four paces around on its outer side. These were probably the foundation stones of a circular cairn or perhaps a dwelling.

The legacies of Stone Age man so far found in Llangollen are twofold. First, there is the axe-hammer found on the lane from Bryn Oerog towards Trevor Hall (1908), manufactured at the Graiglwyd Factory at Pennmaenmawr. Second, another axe-hammer of quite a different shape (eight inches long) found in 1948 in a field in the Pengwern valley by Mr. L. Sands. This was described as a *greywack* and was probably manufactured in Cornwall. The Grosvenor Museum, Chester has a similar one found in Bala lake in 1884. Another has been found in Cardigan.

As representatives of Bronze Age civilisation we have five bronze axe-heads; four found on Dinas Brân and one on Fron Fawr. Ferrets bring them out of rabbit holes or a plough turns them up.

Bronze Age axehead found on Dinas Brân.

In 1879, the tumulus above Dinbren Ucha was partially opened and the late Mr. James Clark, in a letter to the *Oswestry Advertiser* dated 30th November 1904, confirmed the finding of a unburned clay urn containing bones. Also in this area, but in the direction of Garth, are to be found a seven-foot monolith (leaning low to the west) and a standing stone five to six feet in height. Here then, within a few hundred yards of each other, you can see the four characteristic monuments of the Stone Age — tumulus, cairn, standing stone and circle.

Before changing its course, the River Dee once flowed along the Pengwern Valley, easy to visualise during periods of very wet weather should one choose to gaze down into it from the top of an adjacent hill. What may seem less credible is that remnants of perhaps one of the earliest dwellings in the area is to be found here — Plas Pengwern.

On 28th May 934 a Saxon charter was made out at Winchester and witnessed by Hywel the Good and 'Tudor'. Tudor is surmised to have been Tudor Trefor, an ancestor of the family based on Pengwern.

The vaulted hall (in use as a dairy), Old Pengwern Hall

An exterior view of Old Pengwern Hall.

This family has continued to this very day to take a leading part in Welsh affairs. In the *Doomsday Book*, a descendant, also called Tudor, is recorded as paying to Earl Roger of Shrewsbury an annual rent of £4.5.0 for Nanheudwy. Whatever portions of their lands this family lost to the Normans, they always retained the township of Pengwern. The first member of this family actually described as living in Pengwern is Bleddyn (1150) and the family continued to hold it under the Princes of Powys Fadog until 1282. Several members of the family held the office of Seneschal to these Princes, so that Dinas Brân and Pengwern were in close communication.

Iorwerth of Pengwern, for instance, witnessed the charter given by Prince Madoc to Valle Crucis in 1234, and his son Iorwerth witnessed charters for Madoc's son and grandsons. This Iorwerth married Catrin, the sister of Llewelyn the last Prince of Wales. They had a son, Einion who, in 1278, was one of eight hostages (all young men of noble Welsh families) were delivered up at the Church of the Holy Cross, Chester, in case Llewelyn should thereafter bear arms against the King.

Einion had an elder brother, Iorwerth, who, in spite of the part he played against the King, was pardoned of any trespasses he was said to have committed. Lands formerly held under the Princes of Powys were now held under the Marcher Lords of Chirk and in 1300 Iorwerth rose in arms against Roger Mortimer, probably because of his conversion of pasturage into forest. Again, he was only fined for trespass. He married Gwladys, who claimed descent in a direct male line from the ancient house of Powys — the dynasty recorded on Eliseg's Pillar.

Their youngest son, Madoc, established the family at Brynkinallt. It is interesting to find that their eldest son, Ednyfed Gam, held a similar appointment to the Marcher lords as his forefathers had held to the lords of Dinas Brân. There is a record of his expenses incurred travelling from Chirk to Wigmore, including payments for servants and horses. The journey occupied four days.

Ednyfed's most famous grandson was Ieuan, who anglicised his name to 'John' and took the surname 'Trevor'. It was the opinion of the late Lord Mostyn that this surname was first 'Trefawr' — the *tref* on *vill* of *awr,* the latter being the name of several of Tudor's descendants. In 1386 he was Precentor of Bath and Wells and in 1389 he became Bishop of Saint Asaph and had a King's Licence to go to Rome and secure the Pope's confirmation. However, on his arrival he found that Urban the VI had already made an appointment to the See of Saint Asaph, but he did invite Tudor to become auditor at the Papal palace. When Saint Asaph became vacant again in 1394 he secured the appointment.

It was now the time of the Wars of the Roses. The Bishop joined the Lancastrians and became a member of the Commission which would go on to depose King Richard II. King Henry IV sent him to Spain to announce the coronation. Nevertheless, he strongly opposed the statute which debarred the Welsh from holding office and warned Parliament of the danger of driving the Welsh to extremities. When Owain Glyndwr burnt Saint Asaph Cathedral and the Bishop's Palace, he declined financial aid from the Archbishop of Canterbury. John Trevor was a Welshman at heart and his brother Adda had married Owain's sister. One summer's day in 1404, Trevor mounted his horse and joined Owain Glyndwr. Thereafter, Owain used him as an ambassador to the French and he is believed to have died in Rome in 1410.

Towards the end of the 14th century a remarkable man, Ieuan Fychan, was born at Pengwern. His father was Ieuan ap Adda and his mother was the first cousin to Owen Tudor, a grandfather of Henry VII. Ieuan Fychan was a man of remarkable physique — soldier, scholar, sportsman, angler and patron of bards (of whom the chief was Guto'r Glyn). He was himself a poet and once combined his versifying and angling by writing a humorous ode to John Eyton in which he begs for a coracle. However, Ieuan's historical importance lay in his marriage — his bride was Angharad, sole heiress of Hywel Tudor of Mostyn in Flintshire. The owners of Pengwern were henceforth lords of Mostyn. It became customary for the head of the family to spend the summer at Pengwern and the winter at Mostyn. Pengwern remained in the hands of the Mostyn family until the beginning of the 19th century, when the various farms from Rhos Pengwern to Ty Isa (now Tyndwr Farm) were sold at auction.

The sale took place at the Hand Inn, Llangollen on Thursday 1st October 1807 as "comprising the whole township of Pengwern within a ring fence — being suitable for a genteel family". The total area of land was held to be 609 acres.

The Pillar of Eliseg. Rowlandson's drawing of 1797. Courtesy National Library of Wales.

Eliseg's Pillar

Eliseg's Pillar stands in a field near the Abbey on the right-hand side of the Ruthin Road, giving its name to the valley and hence to the Abbey. To understand its significance one must go back a little in history.

The Romans had left Wales by 400AD. The Anglo-Saxons were soon conquering the south east of Britain, but the Celtic peoples still occupied Cornwall, Wales, Lancashire and right up to the river Clyde. However, the Scoti came from Ireland and invaded North Wales. Had they remained we would now be speaking Irish instead of Welsh. Instead, the heroic Cundda and his sons left the Firth of Forth for Gwynedd and expelled the Irish settlers, setting up their own kingdoms in Denbighshire. By this time, however, the Kingdom of Powys — of which the Llangollen area forms so interesting a part — was already in being when Aethelfrith came down from his kingdom in Yorkshire. He annexed part of Cumberland in 604AD and pushed on towards Chester, defeating the Welsh in battle and massacred the monks of Bangor Is Y Coed in 613AD. In this battle the Welsh were led by Selyf of Powys, a member of the ruling family that governed and united Powys for two hundred and fifty years (600–850AD) and the King who had the Pillar erected was the last of that reigning family. He died on a pilgrimage to Rome in the year 854AD so the Pillar must, therefore, have been erected before that year.

Eliseg's Pillar is unique in Britain. It remained erect and entire until the time of the Civil War before being noticed by some of Cromwell's men who happened to be passing by. Thinking it to be a Popish cross, they eagerly smashed it down, breaking the Pillar — formally some twelve feet high, but presently standing at a little more than eight. There is a similar-shaped cross in Corwen churchyard, but this is not inscribed. There is another at Gosforth, in Cumberland, which has a contemporary inscription, but the cross erected by Concenn bears no fewer than thirty-one lines of Latin minuscules, certain letters of which can still be deciphered when noonday sun shines on the Pillar.

It was indeed fortunate that Edward Lhuyd passed by in 1696, when the inscription could still be read. The ends of many of the lines had been broken off but Lhuyd transcribed all that was left — a considerable amount. His transcription was photographed for Sir John Rhys for his article in the *Cymmrodor* in 1908. The writer of the inscription, Commarch, states that the King had it erected to the memory of his great-grandfather Eliseg, who saved the inheritance of Powys from the English and that Concenn had secured another eleven thousand acres for Powys.

Eliseg's Pillar after restoration by Thomas Lloyd of Trevor Hall.

> CONCENN FILIUS CATELI. CATELI FILIUS
> BROCKMAIL BROCKMAIL FILIUS ELISEG
> ELISEG FILIUS CNOILLAINE CONCENN
> ITAQUE PRONEPOS ELISEG EDIFICAVIT
> HUNC LAPIDEM PROAVO SUO ELISEG

A reasonable translation of which would be:
> CONCENN, THE SON OF CATELI; CATELI SON OF BROCHMAIL; BROCHMAIL,
> THE SON OF ELISEG; ELISEG, THE SON OF CNOILLAINE; CONCENN, THEREFORE
> THE GREAT-GRANDSON OF ELISEG, ERECTED THIS STONE TO HIS GREAT-
> GRANDFATHER ELISEG.

Concenn was the last of that dynasty of Powys. His sister, Nest, married Merfyn the Manxman, and their son Rhodri Fawr (Roderick the Great) became the King of Powys and founded the second reigning house. The extent of the Kingdom of Powys varied at different periods and at its greatest extended from Hope in Flintshire as far as Machynlleth. It was divided into *commotes* and those appropriate here are *Yale* and *Nanheudwy*. Today, when we speak of Yale, one thinks of the Llandegla-Bryneglwys area but through many centuries Yale's boundary was the River Dee. It thus included the Castle, the Abbey and a section of modern Llangollen. Nanheudwy's southern boundary was the Ceiriog and it included the Church and towns of Llangollen and Chirk.

The Pillar lay broken on the ground for more than a century, until the Reverend John Price, Bodleian Librarian and uncle of Doctor Price of Llangollen, wrote to the landowner Trevor Lloyd esquire of Trevor Hall. He tactfully expressed the hope that Mr. Lloyd might see fit to restore the monument, which he was — mercifully — pleased to do. Fortunately, the base of the column had survived the ravages of time and Cromwell and was given the following inscription:

> LA CRUCIS QUOD HUJUS VETERIS MONUMENTI SUPEREST DIU
> EX OCULIS REMOTUM ET NEGLECTUM TANDEM RESTITUIT
> T. LLOYD TREVOR HALL, MDCCLXXIX

Which translates as:

*T. Lloyd, of Trevor Hall, at length, in the year
1779, restored what remains of this ancient monument,
Which has been a long time removed from sight, and neglected.*

W.T. Simpson, who wrote a guide to Llangollen in 1827, interviewed the men who had been employed in resetting it. One of these, a very old man (huntsman to Mr. Lloyd) recalled the incident clearly. He said, "there was a large silver coin found in the coffin, which he kept; but that the skull was gilded to preserve it and was then again deposited with its kindred bones. I asked if the bones were sound, and he answered (I give his own words) 'O, no Sir; they broke like gingerbread' We can assume that they were the remains of King Eliseg".

It is also interesting to note the method employed when interring the body some twelve hundred years ago:

"On digging below the flat pedestal in which the base of the Pillar had been inserted they came to a layer of pebblestones; and after having removed them, to a large flat slab, on which it seems the body had been laid, as they now found the remains of it, guarded round with large flat blue stones, and covered at the top with same; the whole forming a sort of stone box or coffin. The bones were entire and of very large dimensions. The skull and teeth, which were very white and perfect, were particularly, sound. By this it would seem that Eliseg was not an old man when he was buried here."

A full description of the Pillar is given in the following extract of a letter, written by the aforementioned Edward Lhuyd (1660–1709) (sometimes spelt *Llwyd* or even *Lloyd*!). He was a famed antiquarian and Celtic scholar, educated at Jesus College, Oxford and he was Keeper of the Ashmolean Museum from 1690 to 1709. As far as is known, he was not a kinsman of the Lloyds of Trevor Hall. This letter was written from Swansea on 14th September 1696, shortly after having visited Llangollen, its recipient being Dr. John Mill (1645–1707), Principal of St. Edmund Hall, Oxford:

"The monument was a stately pillar of very hard stone, of the same kind with our common millstone. It was of a cylindrical form, above twelve feet in height, seven in circumference at the basis, where it is thickest, and about six at the top, where it was smallest. The pedestal is a large stone, five feet square and fifteen inches thick; in the midst whereof there is a round hole, wherein the monument was placed. Within a foot of the top, it is encompassed with a round band or girth, resembling a cord, from whence it is square to the top, and meeting at the corners. It was erected on a small mount, which seems to have been cast up for that purpose; but in the late civil wars (or sooner) it was thrown down and broken into several pieces. It is remarkable that, adjoining the monument, there is a township called Eglwyseg, which is doubtless corrupted from this Eliseg, though our greatest critics interpret it Terra Ecclesiastica."

Now, surrounded by iron railings and protected by CADW, Eliseg lies undisturbed.

A 19th century artist's impression of Castell Dinas Brân.

Castell Dinas Brân

Dinas Brân Castle rises within a triple ring of earthworks once occupied by men of the Bronze Age. The site, a top of a conical hill, about 1100ft above sea level, was too good to be neglected by later generations and it was occupied by the Princes of Powys. The original buildings, probably more than one, were of wood. The castle was destroyed by fire in the 10th century and, as we shall see, was rebuilt.

There is a stream running along the north base of the castle hill, down past the house called 'The Tower', under the canal, road and railway and joining the Dee near the house called 'Sunnydale'. Its name is 'Bran', but whether the stream was named after the castle or the castle after the stream, is a moot point.

W.T. Simpson records the following legend as to how the castle got its name. At his death a certain Duke of Cornwall left his kingdom to his twin sons, Beli and Brân. Disagreements arose between them and a day was finally appointed to decide their various claims by force of arms.

However, their mother, Queen Corwena, called both her sons to her apartments and made so pathetic an appeal to them to throw down their arms and live in peace, that they there and then dismissed their armies. Beli went to New Troy (London) and Brân took up his residence in a fortress, which he had built near Llangollen and called Dinas Brân after his own name. The Queen returning to the portion of land which had been given to her as a jointure, and there she built a small town, which she named Corwen.

Leaving legend now for facts, one of the greatest rulers of Powys, Gruffydd Maelor I, had his favourite residence in Dinas Brân. He died there in 1191 and his body was carried with pomp and ceremony for burial in Meifod, Montgomeryshire, whose church

Castell Dinas Brân. An arial view showing the triple earthworks which date from the Bronze Age.

contains many interesting relics of the ancient line of Powys. It would be interesting to ascertain the route by which this princely funeral procession reached Meifod from Llangollen.

At Gruffydd's death Powys was divided into two: *Powys Fadog* (northern) and *Powys Wenwynwyn* (southern). *Powys Fadog*, containing Yale and Nanheudwy, fell to Madog ap Gruffydd who built the present castle. He was also the founder of Valle Crucis Abbey. Perhaps he was imitating his cousin who ruled southern Powys for he, just a few years previously, had built Dolforwyn Castle, which is of the same design as Dinas Brân and also of Strata Marcella Monastery. However, Madoc's buildings have lasted longer than those of his cousin, for there is little left of Dolforwyn and nothing at all of Strata Marcella. Quite obviously, there must have been a structure here before Madoc began building, as well as an even earlier one said to have been destroyed by fire in the 10th century. Both would certainly have been wooden halls.

Madoc died in 1236 and his son, Gruffydd Maelor II, inherited the new stone Castle. A legend that long held the field states that upon his death in 1270 Gruffydd left two infant sons, Llewelyn and Gruffydd, as his heirs. He was buried at the side of his father in the Abbey Church of Valle Crucis.

It was claimed these sons were (upon the direction of Edward I) made wards of Earl Warren of Holt and Roger Mortimer of Chirk who conspired to have them secretly drowned under Holt Bridge. The dastardly deed was said to have been carried out by Earl Warren himself, their estates conveniently reverting to their guardians. In fact, all four sons survived Gruffydd Maelor II with all of them inheriting some share of their

An early 19th century romantic view of Dinas Brân from the River Dee. From an original painting in the author's collection.

father's domains. Madoc, the eldest, had Dinas Brân for his residence and Gruffydd, far from being drowned, became an ancestor of Owain Glyndwr.

Edward I's conquest of Wales put an end to the kingdom of Powys Fadog. The portion of Yale, which included Dinas Brân and Valle Crucis, went with Chirkland and from now on adherents of the Mortimers and Arundels inhabited the castle. In fact, it became a mere appendage of Chirk Castle. This is why the charming old roadway past the Three Trees and Tyndwr became so important.

It was during the time of the Arundels at Chirk that a branch of the Trevor family, surname Vychan, occupied Dinas Brân. To them was born the beautiful Myfanwy, who was loved by a humble bard, Hywel ap Einion. "Fair as the driven snow on the Arans or as the flower of the Cherry and Hawthorn", so said the poet who loved her and hid his verses in the cleft of an oak tree on the slope of Dinas Brân. Hywel was born in 1330, and his poem is included in the Myrvian Archialogy. This links the 14th and 19th centuries, for Ceiriog won a Silver Crown at the Llangollen 1858 Eisteddfod for his poem 'Myfanwy Fychan' The tender depths of Hywel's passion, which sadly does not appear to have been wholly reciprocated by Myfanwy, is illustrated in the following extracts from his ode.

O! fairer thou, and colder, too,

Than new fall'n snow on Aran's brow;
O! lovely flower of Trevor race,
Let not a cruel heart disgrace
The beauties of thy heavenly face!
Thou art my daily thought; each night
Presents Myfanwy to my sight.

Ah! Cans't thou, with ungentle eye,
Behold thy faithfull Hywel die?

Alas! No words can speak my pain,
While thus I love, but love in vain.
Wisdom and reason — what are they?
What all the charms of poesy
Against the fury of thy darts,
Thou vanquisher of human hearts?
When first I saw thee, princely maid,
In scarlet robes of state arrayed,
Thy beauties set my soul on fire,
And every motion fann'd desire.
Not half so fine the spiders' thread,
That glitters on the dewy mead,
As the bright ringlets of thy hair,
Thou beauteous object of my care.
But, ah! My sight, my tears, are vain –
The cruel maid insults my pain

In his turn Owain Glyndwr had occasion to storm the castle, thus accounting for its ruined condition. However, there would seem no historical evidence of this. What is true is that for a period of only one year before Owen's rising, Dinas Brân became the property of the King of the Isle of Man! It was given to him after the beheading of Richard Fitzalan, the sixth Earl of Arundel.

By the time of Henry VIII (1506–1552), the castle was indeed in ruins. John Leland, the earliest of modern English antiquaries, observed when visiting sometime after 1534 that "the castle of Dinas Brane was never a bygge thing, but sette al for strenngth in a place half inaccessible for enemies"

He further records that its only inhabitant was an eagle who annually nested there. Sadly, the poor bird was not "inaccessible for enemies" for:

"A person was wont to be lowered in a basket to take the young, and was obliged to have another basket over his head, to save him from the fury of the old bird"

In Victorian days the advent of the railway made Llangollen much more accessible and the town became a favourite resort of holidaymakers. Invading the Castle became a very popular pastime. One of these was the redoubtable George Borrow, who made his ascent in 1854 accompanied, unwontedly, by a posse of local offspring:

"A number of children almost entirely girls, followed me. I asked them why they came after me. 'In the hope that you will give us something', said one in very good English. I told them that I should give nothing, but they still followed me".

19ᵗʰ century tourists making their ascent by donkey.

He eventually completing his ascent, having given on his way the benefit of his wisdom to a group of men cutting hay, and clearly still accompanied, he attempted to enjoy the view, but:

"As I stood gazing around the children danced upon the grass, and sang a song. The song was in English. I descended the hill; they followed me to its foot, and then left me. The children of the lower class of Llangollen are great pests to visitors. The best way to get rid of them is to give them nothing: I followed that plan and was not long troubled with them."

Poor Mr. Borrow! It may be thought that this is the first recorded instance of the commercialisation of Dinas Brân. However, in 1827 Simpson had written that within the ruins ...

"A room has been built within these few years, for the shelter and convenience of visitors to the castle; the key of which may be obtained at a little white cottage [probably Geufron] *half way up the hill, inhabited by a very civil woman of the name of Parry, who conducts the visitants, and provides them with tea if required."*

This venture would seem to have been short lived, as in 1845 we read that the room had lain in ruins for some years. However, by the 1880s we are informed by Hugh Jones that:

"There is a neat, ornamental cottage on the summit, which was built some years ago by Mr. Samuel Jones, in which he and his jolly wife Mrs. Jones reside all the year round. Rations are supplied here at very reasonable terms, and parties carrying their own provisions receive every attention."

The summit of Dinas Brân showing the camera obscura and shop on the extreme right.

What stamina the attendant couple must have possessed! One would have had to carry all supplies, even water, to the summit by hand or by donkey with panniers. There was a well at the top but at this time it was recorded as being choked with rubbish. For those who did not wish to make the ascent on foot donkeys could be had for hire at the foot of the hill. The charge was one shilling per donkey. Up until the Second World War there was still one donkey making his daily journey with supplies for the little shop before being pensioned-off to Rhyl beach where he carried delighted children along the sands.

The more energetic could buy a walking stick. For many years an old lady advertised her aids to the pedestrian with the mixed couplet:

Tir Glas is very slippy
Pric and ffon is very handy.

Welsh being her first language, a reasonable translation would be:

Green sward is very slippery
Stick and staff is very handy.

The little shop built by Mr. Samuel Jones was eventually taken over by Miss. E.A. Roberts, daughter of the [then] bakery shop at 39 Church Street. Her parents apprenticed her to a dressmaker — a training she heartily disliked — and she eventually prevailed upon her father to lend her the princely sum of £10 to start her enterprise on Dinas Brân.

It took four years before she was able to make enough profit to repay the loan, but she reigned for over forty-five years as 'Queen of the Castle' where she provided teas and chocolate, biscuits and oranges.

There were also penny-in-the slot machines and mechanical toys plus the wonders of the *camera obscura*, which she operated with much skill. The latter being, in simple terms, a rotating, focusing lens which transferred the picture onto a viewing screen and was the direct antecedent of the early photographic camera. The mechanism was housed in an octagonal metal structure anchored to the ground by guy-ropes of steel wire. From a distance it had the appearance of a giant dustbin or garden incinerator. From such a position as the summit of Dinas Brân, it was possible to get a detailed panorama of the surrounding countryside.

Sometimes rather too detailed! It is amusing to recall the story of a local grand lady who, in order to entertain her guests, proposed a gentle ascent of Dinas Brân followed by the entertainment provided by *camera obscura*. The day being very fine, there was certain to be a clear view of all about them. Too clear, in fact! To her great consternation and the embarrassment of her guests, the camera strayed upon a vision of her daughter, to be seen reclining in the heather in the company of the local curate. We shall not name the parties involved but it was significant that said curate was quickly banished to a punishment parish!

Miss Peggy Chubb and pet dog in front of the shop during the mid-1930s.

Today, very little remains of Castell Dinas Brân, but it is still possible to identify many features:
- the main entrance at the north east corner,
- the keep at the south east corner,
- the gothic windows of the banqueting hall in the south wall which joins ...
- the remains of a square tower of characteristic Welsh design.

Note also the circular dungeon and narrow passageway. For many years the castle was leased from the Chirk Castle estate by the Llangollen Town Council for a peppercorn rent. It is now in the care of CADW.

The useful little shop is long gone as is the *camera obscura*, blown away in a great gale more than forty years ago. Even the tall flagpole, which so proudly flew *Y Ddraig Goch*, has disappeared without trace. Let the last word be left to Roger Cyffyn, a Welsh bard, who wrote:

> *"Gone are thy gates Dinas Brân on the height!*
> *Thy wardens are blood-crows and ravens, I trow;*
> *Now no one will wend from the field of the fight*
> *To the fortress on high save the Raven and Crow."*

... and the stout-booted, camera-clicking tourist of course.

A rare and unusual late 18th century view of Valle Crucis Abbey. Artist unknown.

Valle Crucis Abbey

In 1200 Madoc ap Gruffydd Maelor, Prince of Powys, "inspired with the love of God and solicited by Peter the Abbot, Diniawel of Strata Florida, Rhirid of Cwmtir and Philip of Strata Marcella, gave to God and Mary the Virgin and the order, Llynegwystl".

Thus was founded the Cistercian Monastery of Llan Egwest, or Valle Crucis, in a lovely and sequestered valley some two miles distant from Llangollen, close to Eliseg's Pillar (from which the area took its name). The Cistercian Order was founded in France in 1098 and their brothers in Wales were notable sheep farmers and known as the 'White Brothers' (the name coming from the colour of their habits which were woven from the wool of their sheep).

Valle Crucis is the best preserved of their Welsh abbeys and with it went the land owning and manorial rights, alongside later endowments as far as Corwen and Wrexham. One of the townships of Wrexham is still known as Wrexham Abbot. Hafod yr Abat on the far side of the Horseshoe Pass and Allt y Bady (leading to the Ceiriog Valley) are names which recall the extent of the Abbey domains.

The *Red Book of Saint Asaph* confirmed the grant of Wrexham and also records in 1234 the right given to the monks to fish in the River Dyfrdwy, the Dee as we know it today. Fishing rights would seem to have been jealously guarded since earliest times.

The monks were greedy and erected 'new works' on the river, thereby allowing them to procure far more fish than the freemen of Llangollen considered to be their fair proportion. This led to a dispute between town and Abbey. It was decided that the Abbot and five monks of the freemen's own choice should decide the matter. Madoc and his secretary appointed a date for the hearing and the assembly was duly held. Regardless of oaths having being solemnly taken, the Abbot and monks found in favour of themselves! Somehow not suprisingly!

But the Llangollen people were not to be easily subjugated. It is said that they sought the intervention of the Pope in the dispute and, as a result, Bishop Trevor was prevailed upon to cause the building of the Town Bridge by way of appeasing the freemen. Firm evidence of this has, however, yet to be found.

The Cistercians of Valle Crucis, although meant to be a silent order, quickly tired of such strictures. Politics were entered into and soon there were land disputes with other abbeys. It would seem that in the age-old fight between God and Mammon, God lost a certain amount of ground.

The philosophy of the simple life would also appear to have held little appeal. There were bards kept, and bards visiting. The hospitality of the Abbey was renowned. Guttyn Owain records that four courses of meat would regularly be served on dishes of bright silver, accompanied by fine clarets.

According to the *Sebright Manuscripts*, Abbot John was seen to bless the poor (and others) "with his three fingers covered with rings". So much for the vow of poverty!

Abbot David ap Iorwerth had his personal bard, Guto'r Glyn, who among other gifts, received a buckle and sword from his patron upon whom he was wont to shower the greatest praise. Upon his death in 1503 Guto'r was buried within the precincts of Valle Crucis. It is estimated that a hundred and nineteen of his poems are extant today!

Abbot John Lloyd, one of the commissioners ordered to draw up the pedigree of Henry VII, was appointed to Valle Crucis in 1480. He was one of three appointed to reform the Welsh abbeys but good though his intentions were, he seems to have had little lasting success here.

Robert of Salisbury became Abbot in 1528 and the following year a case of wrongdoing was brought against him by one John Vaughn, eventually going to Chancery. This led to an investigation of the Abbey's affairs conducted by the Abbot of Neath and three others.

We next hear of him some seven years later in Oxfordshire, having been accused of robbery and the minting of base metal coins, in partnership with a goldsmith by the name of Hall. Both men

The west front, c.1900.

East view of the Abbey by the Buck brothers dated 1742.

West view of Valle Crucis Abbey by Nathaniel and Samuel Buck, 1742.

were committed to the Tower, a long way from the pleasures of life in the Vale of the Cross.

The last Abbot, John Heron, was appointed in 1530. In no time at all, and for reasons of his own, he had arranged a lease of the manor of Wrexham plus an annuity, to Sir William Penyson. A misuse of church lands which resulted in chancery proceedings in 1533.

Wrexham was originally an agricultural pastoral parish of almost 2,000 acres, spread over fourteen townships. In 1220 this was partly appropriated to Valle Crucis Abbey by Bishop Reyner of Saint Asaph and solely by his successor in 1227.

By now it would seem that Valle Crucis had gained the reputation of being the most corrupt abbey in Wales and the fabric of the building was also beginning to decay.

In August 1535, Henry VIII's commissioners spent four days at the Abbey, taking an inventory preparatory to its dissolution. Their report showed the house to be in great need of reform. Abbot Heron was taken to Holt Castle on 15th September when it was decided that he was to be relieved of his office. Only six monks remained within this vast house, none of them considered fit to be appointed as Abbot.

The Abbey Church was found to be in great need of repair and in debt to the King and others to the tune of 300 Marks. Valle Crucis was one of the first abbeys to be closed and its value at the time of dissolution (1535) was shown to be only one hundred and eighty eight pounds and five shillings. Curiously, Heron was given a pension of £25 per annum which he was still drawing twenty years later!

The Abbey and its adjacent lands were henceforth in the gift of the Crown. James I gave them to his envoy Lord Wolton, from whom they passed to his daughter Margaret in 1654. She was a recusant, refusing to attend the services of the Church of England, and Oliver Cromwell put the property under seques-tration to Edward Davies, Master Shearer, of Eglwyseg.

Sunshine and shadow. The Chapterhouse passage, 1930.

John Trevor (1620–1683) of Trevor Hall acquired the property by purchase. From him they were inherited by his daughter Mary who, through her marriage, established the Lloyd family of Trevor Hall. From them, by direct inheritance, the Abbey and its lands passed to the Hughes family of Coed Helen estate, Caernarfon, who retained ownership until 1949 when it came into the care of the [then] Ministry of Works and now CADW.

The well-preserved ruins we find today are comprised in the Abbey Church and eastern range of claustral buildings.

The Church, following the standard plan on the Cistercian order, is cruciform in plan and would almost certainly have been built with the aid of freemasons who were incorporated about this time and were the chief contractors for buildings of this sort. They travelled from county to county and, when they found religious houses needing to be built, camped on site. Freemasons are credited with the introduction of the cruciform style for ecclesiastical buildings.

The west front is particularly fine and was captured in a wonderfully romantic painting by J.M.W. Turner, now lodged in the British Museum. Entry is gained through double doors set in a richly ornamented arch. Above this a fine window consisting of three lancet arches above that again is a circular rose window of eight divisions and great beauty. Over the rose window are the eroded remains of the following inscription:

> *"A.D. – Adam – Dus fecit hoc opus*   *The Abbot Adam did this work.*
> *Pace Beata quiescat. Amen."*   *May he rest in happy peace. Amen.*

The aisled nave is five bays in length, the east end having three rather curious lower windows arranged with a further two above and executed in quite different architectural style to that of the west end.

Among the claustral and other buildings is a well-preserved chapterhouse with dormitories above. Parts of the [ruined] adjoining apartments west and south have also been revealed.

The entire Abbey complex is beautifully kept — grass neatly cut and everything in its place. A far cry from the romantic, ivy-clad, rook-haunted buildings of the writer's childhood, and one cannot help feeling that something magical has been lost. Visitors are advised to avert their gaze from the adjacent caravan site and its attendant activity. Hardly the most compatible of neighbours, but playing its part in the task of keeping farming afloat.

Past visitors found it a more sequestered spot. And visitors there were aplenty! After its dissolution, Valle Crucis quickly fell into decay and eventual ruin. Local people came to see what they could usefully find, taking away fallen stones and timbers to be used elsewhere. Many old buildings within the Llangollen area claim to have bits of the Abbey incorporated within the fabric.

It was a long-held belief that the magnificent roof of the parish Church came from the Abbey, the same claim having been made for an impressive brass chandelier, which still hangs in Trevor Church.

As far as the roof is concerned, the expert Dr. Thomas places this as 15th century work and would have been completed while the Abbey was still intact.

However at Porkington (now known as *Brogyntyn*), the fine Georgian mansion and seat of Lord Harlech, the saloon had a curious painting, formerly part of the altarpiece. The whereabouts of this are not known today and the present Lord Harlech, due to financial strictures has been forced to abandon the mansion in favour of a smaller house on the estate.

For much of the 18th and 19th centuries, Valle Crucis was used as a farmhouse with many of the claustral buildings housing livestock.

During the 18th and 19th centuries it became fashionable among the gentry to seek-out 'romantic ruins' in picturesque situations. Small parties of acquaintances descended on the ruins, normally led by a 'knowledgeable' gentleman sporting a fashionable walking cane with which he would point and poke about.

For most of this period the chapter-house and rooms above were used as a farmhouse. A contemporary traveller complained of the dormitories having being converted into a hayloft and the vaulted cloister, supported by rows of low pillars, divided into compartments — these appropriated for cattle. The area covered by the Abbey Church was much overgrown with tall ash trees. It was customary for the farmer's wife to receive the visiting parties and offer such refreshment as was appropriate, for which she hoped to be suitably rewarded. Within the grounds, situated at the head of the Abbot's fishpond, there was also a neat 18th century summerhouse with

The Abbot's fishpond and 18ᵗʰ century summer pavilion.

The east end and Abbot's fishpond in the late 18ᵗʰ century. Artist unknown.

imposing bay window, built by the Lloyds of Trevor Hall for the summer entertainment of their family and friends.

Soon after its erection this was described in the summer of 1773 as being a charmingly attractive summer pavilion, surmounted by a gilded ball. The fishpond was fenced around with a neat, bright green railing constructed in the Chinese style.

When W.T. Simpson visited in 1827 he found this arrangement somewhat less charming and refers to "a kind of summer house at the back of the Abbey, joining a pond abounding with trout. Here was a charming field for the display of taste; but, as in the hut at the top of Dinas Brân, the opportunity has been lost". This proves once again that acceptable taste is a very personal thing!

The golden ball and *chinoiserie* railing had obviously disappeared by then, thus escaping Mr. Simpson's wrath. The summerhouse survived, later becoming the custodian's official residence (when such a person was finally appointed in the 19th century). In 1837 a certain Ann Dale held this office. In that year she was a mere seventy-seven years of age!

She was succeeded by Miss Jane Lloyd. Something of a mystery figure and obviously not without means, being able to keep a maidservant, Mary Elizabeth Williams. Also, upon her death in November 1881, she left £200 — a princely sum for those days — for the restoration of Llangynog parish Church from which village she is thought to have hailed.

George Borrow visited in 1854 and was clearly impressed — and intrigued — by Miss Lloyd. Describing her as initially cross and lofty, but later becoming kind and communicative, showing him her cottage from which she went away in winter to such places as Harrogate and the Isle of Wight (information which she did not, however, disclose to him).

Borrow thought there to be "something singular about her" and believed "she had a history of her own". Quite true, apparently. He described her as being "genteelly dressed, about the middle age, rather tall and bearing in her countenance the traces of beauty". Jane Lloyd continued in the office of custodian of Valle Crucis until her death and kept quite detailed accounts peppered with her personal comments upon some of the visitors whom, it would seem, she always personally accompanied about the ruins. For many years these accounts and other of her papers were lodged in the offices of Charles Richards & Sons, Llangollen, a long-established firm of solicitors.

Visitors gained entry to the Abbey by ringing a bell operated by chain pull at the west door and it would seem that there was, at that time, no set charge for admission — it being left to the individual to reward as he thought fit.

William Gladstone gave twelve shillings, although it would seem that one twelfth of this was more usual. Anything less was deemed unacceptable. All in all, Miss Lloyd appears to have enjoyed an average income of about £80 per annum. But there were always those who chose not to pay anything at all and this incurred her wrath! Others would clamber over the wall or "scamp over rails". Soon after her departure, a standard entrance fee of sixpence was introduced.

The Reverend H.T. Owen, a keen archaeologist, succeeded Jane Lloyd. During the summer of 1888 his investigations in the monk's dormitory revealed five sepulchral slabs beneath a depth of accumulated earth. The following year he turned his attentions to the north transept and aisle, unearthing plinths and buttresses, which were found to be in remarkably good condition. Importantly, he also discovered a stone, some five and a half-feet long, depicting the double-handed sword of Knights Templar.

He also found some beautiful examples of 13th century stained glass, a few tiles and several pieces of molten lead, being remnants of the fire of the 1240s, after which that section of the Abbey Church had to be rebuilt.

Something the Reverend Owen did not discover was a gold noble of Henry VI, of very fine workmanship found in a ditch beyond the cloisters on May 7th 1959. An inquest on the coin was held in Llangollen in July and it is now in the possession of the National Museum, Cardiff who kindly loaned it for display at the Llangollen Historical Exhibition of 1960.

It would seem that Reverend Owen was strangely absent in the very hot summer of 1903 when the Abbey was visited by the author of *Pilgrimages to Old Homes*, Fletcher Moss, accompanied as always by his stalwart friend, the photographer 'X'!

"We found it locked up and no-one there. A notice on the grand entrance told us to ring the bell and pay sixpence if we had a camera. But we nearly broke the bell and no one came. So after a careful inspection of the walls and fences, we left our bicycles, set up the camera, and I climbed the wall, pulled up the camera, and X followed".

Naughty boys — Jane Lloyd would have dealt with them severely. Inside they found a peaceful, lovely place with Madonna Lilies among the finest ever seen. The monk's pool full of fat fish and in the Abbey well a big trout partly hidden under a stone.

One of the eleven skeletons in what must have been the monks' burial ground, disturbed when the Abbey was occupied as a farm in the 19th century.

"We had a drink of that cold water, and were told afterwards that if the Reverend caretaker had been home, he would have charged us two pence a cup for it. We thought of leaving sixpence for photographing the well, but someone might have wondered if the trout had done it and had any more."

Valle Crucis has a special place among the happier memories of the writer's childhood. In company with most other places it suffered a certain amount of neglect during the Second World War and had become populated with ivy, trees and undergrowth. Altogether a much more romantic, natural place which seemed to grow out of the ground rather than stand upon it, as does the well-preserved and ordered ruin of today.

The curator was Mrs. Polly Roberts, considered a great friend by my sister and I. We spent many hours in her willing guardianship. Our parents, *en route* to assignations of their own, would leave us at the top of the lane by the old covered well and we would run eagerly down to the west door, clutching our sixpences. The first one there would ring the bell, which clanged merrily when the long chain was pulled. Eventually Mrs. Roberts would appear, never failing to welcome us — and rarely taking the proffered sixpence.

And then the freedom of the place was ours, with so much to do and explore! Only the Abbey Church and the area in front of the chapterhouse were regularly maintained. Summer growth and self-seeded shrubbery added to the air of mystery and excitement. Largely ruined buildings and fragments of walls lurked amid all this, an area where the average tourist chose not to stray. Behind the east window there was a great patch of more than waist-high stinging nettles — this was generally avoided. Close by stood the charming little curator's cottage where, at quiet times, we would be given lemonade and rosy-red apples. The cottage was so arranged as to have sitting and bedrooms upon the upper level approached by a short flight of external stone steps. Below, in a semi-basement, was the kitchen-living room.

Sometimes, on warm sunny days, an old man would sit outside with a tame jackdaw upon his shoulder. This had suffered a broken wing and owed its life to his having adopted it.

Some ancient sepia photographs hung in the chapterhouse. Carved stones were placed about the floor and in a shallow, glass-topped case placed within the great window, there reposed some fragments of stained glass and other artefacts as discovered by the Reverend Owen.

For many years, Peter the Dog was Mrs. Roberts' faithful companion and accomplice. Of uncertain parentage, he was largish and amiable with a winning smile. As far as visitors were concerned, his main job was to lure them to the well near the chapterhouse, long since abandoned by the trout. Here he would sit at the head of it while the tourists

An internal view in the 1950s after the ruins had been restored by the Ministry of Works.

were encouraged to toss coins across for him to deftly catch in his mouth and drop into the well. Only silver was acceptable, coppers being treated with contempt. After closing time his mistress would reclaim the coins with a fishing net, always leaving one or two as bait.

In later years Mrs. Roberts scandalised many by partitioning off one corner of the chapterhouse, making a field kitchen for the preparation of much-needed teas for grateful tourists. These were provided with the aid of a cast iron wood and coal burning stove, the chimney disappearing through a corner of the ancient window. Perhaps not the best of ideas — the whole thing was hastily swept away with the coming of the Ministry of Works.

Perhaps the greatest privilege of all was being allowed beyond the 'NO ADMITTANCE' sign. So it read on a narrow door to the left of the west door when viewed from within the Abbey. Beyond it was a small space containing guidebooks, postcards, a canvas-seated deck chair (never known to be put up) and a selection of *impedimenta,* the nature of which the memory fails to recall. At the back was a mysterious spiral stone stair leading upwards. Upon ascending, one was delivered out on to the top of a high, and no doubt crumbling, wall.

From this vantagepoint it was possible to gaze arrogantly down upon lesser visitors, some of whom, having children of their own, would demand that they should be offered the same privilege. Mrs. Roberts summarily dismissed such suggestions. She would tell them: "Those children are special. They are friends of the Abbey!" How smirkily superior we felt. What smug little brats we really were!

Those days alas, were destined to end as childhood gave way to changes and an enforced exile from the area except for frequent visits.

Mrs. Polly Roberts eventually retired to a small, grey cottage at the foot of Hill Street where she passed her remaining days in gentle retirement, regardless of several 'near misses' as a result of having taking to driving rather late in life.

Valle Crucis Abbey of course, seems set to endure forever. *Dei gratia.*

The parish Church soon after the addition of the south aisle in 1863.

The Parish Church

The core of Llangollen lies in the Church and Churchyard. Christianity was introduced into Britain during the Roman occupation and early in the 5th century monasticism extended over the whole country. The monks lived in separate huts or cells, with the cells surrounded by a wall or rampart. Within this wall were also the Church, the Abbot's cell, the hospice and the various outhouses. The whole was known as the 'Llan' or 'enclosure'. Hence the name *Llangollen* means 'Collen's enclosure'.

Collen was a 7th century saint who chose this spot to build his hermitage. As likely or not, he reached here by water transport — in a coracle, such as are still used by fishermen on the Teifi and the Dee.

Curiously, there is no other Church in Wales dedicated to Saint Collen, although Brittany has a village called *Langolen*, whose Church has a statue of him in the garb of an Anchorite. There is, however, *Ffynnon Collen* above Pentredwr, a little to the right of the old road by the Horseshoe Pass. This is where Saint Collen is said to have washed the blood from his arms after slaying the giantess who dwelt in Graig-Arthur opposite World's End.

It is not known exactly when the stone-built Church replaced the original wooden buildings, but the Reverend D.R. Thomas in his *History of the Diocese* is of the opinion that the walls are of Norman workmanship. The Church was an important one, certainly in the 12th century, and was the 'mother Church' for a wide area — a mandate of a Papal Legate dated 8th March 1274 claims that Wrexham, Ruabon, Chirk, Glyn Ceiriog

The parish Church today.

and Llangdegla were from ancient times only Chapels of Llangollen Church.

Unlike the rest of the Church, the original tower is thought to have been added c.1500 after fire severely damaged the building (curiously, on the feast of Saint Collen, May 21st). After this, extensive rebuilding was required. It remained of wooden construction until 1749.

In that year the Rural Dean made a report on the Church fabric. The wooden tower contained three tuneable bells and a clock, but the Dean suggested that a building lying to the west of the tower called the 'Old Church' should be taken down, the stone to be used for building the present tower, which then had four bells and a clock with quarter chimes. In 1887 a peal of eight Jubilee bells was set up and the chimes added to the clock in 1890, as commemorated on the brass plate in the west porch. At the time of the building of the new tower, a gallery designed to seat about one hundred was built at the west end. This is lighted by a dormer window above the south porch.

It was said that the remains of Saint Collen lay in the demolished building which was used for the tower and right up to 1927 there were fragments of an alabaster figure said to be that of Saint Collen. It is said that this figure was removed from the decorated niche in the north aisle. "The unshapely remains of this monument are still to be seen in the belfry where it had been thrown" (W.T. Simpson, 1927). Sadly, there is no record of their present whereabouts, but the certain thing is that they are no longer in the Church.

The Church as it is now dates from 1863, when the south aisle was added, the east end was extended and the west door was put into the tower.

The Vicar at the time was William Edwards, father of the first Archbishop of Wales, and his grave can be seen on the north side of the Churchyard. Originally this grave was surmounted by a cross which, having become very damaged, was removed. The archway entering the nave on the south side is the original north doorway, behind which the choir's vestry was built. Fortunately, there is a watercolour of the Church as it was before the 1863 extensions. It hangs in the Church porch, and it will be seen that the east wall and window were where the chancel steps now are. E.W. Cox painted this c.1850, and the circular window shown above the altar was later incorporated in the building of Eglwyseg Church. Unfortunately, it was accidentally installed with the stained glass reversed, which caused it to deteriorate. In the east window was one of only two Welsh inscriptions in the Church, although at the time the services were read always in Welsh except on the second Sunday in the month. The inscription referred to may be found in Luke 22, Verse 42. There is in addition a Welsh inscription on a roof beam in the north aisle: "Y nav ti Mair vydd Barod Bob awr" — *Heaven for thee Mary will be ready every hour*.

The oak carved roof and ceiling over the pre-1863 sanctuary are the outstanding beauty of the Church. According to D.R. Thomas they are of 15th century construction. In 1931 they were found to be suffering from the attacks of beetles and were brought down for renovation and treatment. At the time of their replacement in 1932 special lighting was put below some of the carvings so that their full beauty could be seen. This has since been replaced with a more efficient installation, which allows one to appreciate the splendid workmanship of this area of the roof.

Until 1876 there had been a north entrance giving access to Church Street, later closed up to allow the building of a sacristy. It is interesting to note that a London Welshman, a Mr. William Griffiths, whose connection with Llangollen was very tenuous (i.e. a friend had been buried in the Churchyard in 1841), met the entire cost.

The west door was not as one might expect, built with the new tower but cut through at the same time as the building of the sacristy to provide a replacement entrance and porch. Altogether a most satisfactory arrangement.

Before going outside, mention must be made of the many fine stained glass windows, which greatly add to the beauty of the building. First, the great east window above the altar. This was the gift of the Tottenham family of Plas Berwyn, in memory of Lady Alicia Tottenham, widow of the Bishop of Clogher. The window has five main lights above which Saint David and Saint Patrick are depicted within the tracery.

The fine Caen stone *reredos* below it was donated by Bamford Hesketh Esq. of Gwrych Castle, Abergele and the news of it greatly disturbed Colonel Tottenham who opposed it, fearing that its erection would detract from the beauty of his window. Llangollen parishioners, being much in favour of the *reredos,* sent a petition to the Ecclesiastical Court at Saint Asaph from whom a ruling had been sought. Colonel Tottenham consequently withdrew his plea, but with the proviso that the height of the *reredos* should be restricted.

It is a matter of regret that similar common sense was not applied in the case of the charming Church of Llantysilio, higher up the valley. Here a much later *reredos* greatly obscures the lower part of the fine east window.

The Hughes-Parry family, formally of Llangollen Fechan, were associated with the town for three centuries and with them is connected the Church's oldest window. This is to be found in the west porch and was donated in 1833 by Margaret, eldest daughter of Thomas Parry.

Other Hughes-Parry windows are to be found in the clergy vestry. Others, one in the east gable of the north aisle and another rather charming one in the north wall, are worth the finding. Also in the north wall is a window commemorating the Diamond Jubilee of Queen Victoria.

In the south wall is a window depicting the Resurrection, erected to the memory of Robert Baker of Plas yn Llan. Close by is another, erected by public subscription, to the memory of General Yorke of Plas Newydd — in which house he is reputed never to have spent a night! Unlike its earlier owners, 'The Ladies of Llangollen', of whom it is said that they never spent a night away from it! Indeed, on the same wall is a monument of singular history in the form of a marble depicting the 'Ladies' Eleanor Butler and Sarah Ponsonby — erected in commemoration by Dr. Mary Gordon in 1937.

Monument to the 'Ladies of Llangollen' commissioned by Dr Mary Gordon in 1937.

Dr. Mary Gordon was one of the first women doctors to be trained in Britain and was medical officer at Holloway Prison at the height of the suffragette demonstrations. She claims to have made contact with 'The Ladies' by use of physic powers, on one occasion having taken the extreme measure of a 'breaking and entering' at Plas Newydd late at night in order to keep an arranged assignation with them in the library of the house. She claimed that the resulting lively and profound conversation she enjoyed with them continued until dawn.

Thereafter, she was inspired to write *The Chase of the Wild Goose*. A largely fictional biography of 'The Ladies' which, having sold moderately well, provided the means with which to commission the monument.

The sculptress was Violet Matthews who depicted herself as Miss Ponsonby, Mary Gordon posing as Lady Eleanor. The dedication was rather a grand affair, the monument being unveiled by Lord Howard de Walden after which it was blessed and dedicated by the Archdeacon. Afterwards, the congregation gathered in the Hand Yard where the sculptress was presented with a large bunch of pink roses.

All this took place in 1937, and Mary Gordon's death occurred quite soon afterwards. We shall now never know the truth of the ghost story as nothing has been heard from Doctor Gordon since her departure.

In more serious vein, between the two stained glass windows on this wall is a simple wooden War Memorial in memory of the one hundred and eleven men from this parish who were cruelly taken in the First World War. Sadly, it was later necessary to extend this memorial in order to include those fifty-five brave men lost to us in the second great conflict (1939-45). It is their right not to be forgotten.

Looking back towards the altar before leaving the Church, the eye is arrested by the impressive wrought-iron chancel screen, which divides it from the main body of the Church. This was the gift of Mrs. Watkin Richards in 1902 and is of excellent workmanship.

Outside in the Churchyard, much local history can be read from the tombstones. To the north of the west door is that of Robert Price, Vicar of Llangollen, 1737–1771, and father of John Price, librarian of the Bodleian for forty-five years, having been born at The Tower below Dinas Brân in 1734.

A little further down is the grave of Edward Jones, the Church clerk whose interesting conversation with George Borrow occupies the eighteenth chapter of *Wild Wales*. He kept a shop in Bridge Street trading as a provision dealer and general merchant and was a person of considerable education.

Near the Hand drive entrance is a stone inscribed with the following interesting lines of verse:

"Our life is but a winter's day;
Some only breakfast and away.
Others to dinner stay and are full fed;
The oldest man but sups and goes to bed.
Large is his debt who lingers out the day,
Who goes the soonest has the least to pay."

Perhaps the most outstanding of all these is the tall, gothic, white marble monument on the south side which marks the last resting place of 'The Ladies' and their faithful maid-companion Mary Carryl (known as 'Molly the Bruiser'). Here, for the first time in their years together, they sleep away from home.

How appropriate the inscription taken from the Book of Job:
"But they shall no longer return to their house neither shall their place know them any more."

Close by is a reasonably new innovation, first thought off some one hundred and twenty years before. The redoubtable Vicar James (1868–1895) had long thought it desirable to make provision for major access from Regent Street in order to provide an "entrance worthy of the Church" He envisaged an impressive lychgate supported at either side by handsome iron railings set upon low stone walls. All very laudable, but somehow it did not happen which is suprising as Enoch Rhys James, BA was renowned for getting his way.

In 1986 half of the National School became available for use as a parish hall and the old schoolyard was, with certain restrictions, made over as much-needed parking spaces for motor cars. It naturally followed that good access to the Churchyard was required here and soon followed the lychgate entrance we see today. Perhaps not as impressive as the arrangement envisaged by Vicar James, but it serves.

The late Mr. J. Iorwerth Roberts, an acclaimed local historian, found that the late Archbishop Edwards claimed to have been told that the old Vicarage stood in the north-west corner of the Churchyard now occupied by part of the Hand Hotel, but was unable to prove the authenticity of this.

Further research has shown that the Vicarage did in fact stand to the south west and probably formed the original part of the building now known as The Grapes Hotel. Before the Victorian additions and improvements (bay windows etc.) this had certainly been an old house. Many will remember the large external chimney breast, which protruded into Hill Street (before being partially demolished by a run-away bulldozer).

It must be remembered that at the time of the Vicarage, Regent Street did not exist and the building would have faced onto one of the main streets of the town — Chapel Street, which continued without dissection into Hall Street.

The Reverend Robert Wynne-Eyton, MA, JP belonged to that now extinct breed — a Squarson — coming from a rich, landed family in Flintshire. If one had a surfeit of sons it was usual to follow the adage 'one for the estate, one for the Church, one for the Army'. Robert was obviously number two and not happy to reside in a house seen to be below his station. In 1816, the year of his arrival, a new Vicarage was built on the north side of the river, south-facing in a semi-rural situation. It is possible that some of his own money was employed in the furbishing of what became probably the grandest town residence of its day. The son of his successor, the Reverend William Edwards described its splendour in some detail, after he became Archbishop of Wales:

Accidental demolition of the external chimney-stack of the original Vicarage, now the Grapes Hotel.

> *"The moment tea was over the boys bounded out to inspect the whole house. Already somewhat enawed by the large entrance hall and dining room, they soon came back to report to my Mother new wonders — such and so many rooms with unheard of names, Morning room, Servants' hall, still-room, pantries, a huge kitchen, larders, laundries and ice-house. One of the boys who penetrated the cellars was puzzled to see wine bottles in what he called bookcases — he had never heard of bins — he had only known wine as a medicine at Llanymawddwy, and he said to my mother that the people who had lived there must have been very often ill, judging by the number of empty bottles. My father and eldest brother had, meanwhile, gone out to survey the gardens and outbuildings, a large flower garden*

Archbishop A.G. Edwards, who so graphically described his arrival at Llangollen Vicarage as a child

and glass houses, stabling for eight horses, coach houses, saddle rooms and granaries."

All this gives us some idea of the style in which Robert Wynne-Eyton lived. He obviously enjoyed considerable private means. When departing Llangollen in 1849, the people of the parish presented him with a fine, solid silver candelabra. The gift pleased him so much that he was moved to have it copied, (in silver-plate, albeit of good quality). For years the pair graced the dining room at Leeswood Hall, Flintshire, until the death of Mrs. H.V. Fairbairn-Wynne-Eyton some twenty years ago.

When the railway line came to Llangollen in 1858, the Vicarage was sold to the Railway Company together with five acres of land for £4,000. A new Vicarage was built with the proceeds, below Fron Bache. Nine acres of glebe land were purchased at the same time. In 1956 this was considered to be too large for modern requirements and was, of course, expensive to maintain. It was sold for as little as £3,500. £2,900 of this was used to buy a 'temporary' Vicarage in the form of a semi-detached, red brick house situated on Abbey Road. This *temporary* arrangement still holds today!

The Rev. Robert Wynne-Eyton's Vicarage, later the Woodlands Hotel.

Llangollen Bridge before demolition of the tower (c.1932).

Llangollen Bridge and the Town

The first object of interest in the town is naturally the Bridge, which can be neither ignored nor avoided. Built in 1345 by John Trevor I of the Pengwern family. He was Bishop of Saint Asaph and resided at Trevor Hall. His father, Iorwerth ap Adda, is buried in the Abbey and his grave-slab is carved to show a half figure in armour with a shield. John Trevor was elevated to the Bishopric in 1352 and he died in 1357. Many confuse him with John Trevor II, also Bishop in his day, but altogether a much more ambitious man. Appointed Precentor of Bath and Wells in 1386, he became Bishop eight years later. Employed by Richard II whom he deserted, later to be made Chamberlain of Chester, Flintshire and North Wales by Henry IV. However, having joined Owain Glyndwr in 1404, he was subsequently forced to flee to Scotland and eventually to France. As far as is known, he never returned to North Wales.

For a very long time Llangollen had the only stone bridge over the Dee. In 1391 it is said that certain tenants in Cefn Mawr paid two shillings a year for the convenience of having a ferryboat across the Dee to take themselves and others to and from Cysyllte and Trevor. Also, the farm named Rhydonnen (*Rhyd* being the Welsh for *ford*) indicates a popular fording of the river above Rhysgog.

It is certain that there had been some sort of structure here before Bishop Trevor's time, and it is almost certain that it would have been of wooden construction. We have much evidence of damage done by the river in spate and such a bridge would be easily disabled or even swept away. The Rolls Patent records a grant of *pontage* from the King to Roger Mortimer in 1284 to be used for the maintenance and repair of his bridge at Llangollen.

Whether an earlier bridge stood upon the same site is a moot point, but rebuilders

Bridge widening in progress in 1969.

Stone mason with a chisel used in the 1873 widening.

since have certainly not deviated. Virtual, but not complete rebuilding took place in 1656. Rondle Reade, the master stonemason left his mark there in the form of a stone inscribed with both his name and the date. The large sum of £250 was officially allotted to this work which indicated that major repairs were required.

Until 1873 Llangollen Bridge was a mere eight feet wide and proved to be inadequate to cope with the increased traffic resulting from 19th century industrial development within and about the town. It was therefore decided to double the width of the carriageway. As is always the case at such times, one or two voices were raised in protest but the majority thought it to be a good thing.

The widening took place on the upriver side, the original being faithfully reproduced. The down-river side remains unaltered to this day. Further widening took place in 1969 — again up river — and allowed for a pedestrian footpath on both sides of the Bridge instead of just one. It is interesting to note that during this work one of the stonemasons used a chisel which had also been employed during the 1873 widening.

Sadly, the excellent work done was marred by the intrusion of unsightly metal railings at the Abbey Road end. This had been first disfigured a decade earlier by the raising of the roadway to provide a square arch to allow the new railway line to pass through. During the course of this work fragments of floriated sepulchral slabs of the sort discovered at the Abbey were found, having been employed as re-cycled building materials.

Bishop Trevor's original bridge, although of stone, had been finished above road level with wooden railings. These were replaced with a stone parapet at the time of the major repair work carried out in 1656. The Abbey, possibly being used as an illicit stone quarry at that time, could well have provided some of the building materials.

By way of compensation for the railway disfigurations, a delicious little folly in the

A coracle fisherman above the old weir.

form of a castellated tower was erected at that end of the Bridge, for many years employed as a confectioner's and teashop. Unfortunately demolished in 1939, this architectural gem was a great loss to the town.

Approximately one hundred years after its advent, the railway fell victim to the infamous Doctor Beeching who sounded the death-knell on one of the countries most scenically beautiful lines — Ruabon to Barmouth. However, the redundant premises took on a new life during the 1968-9 bridge widening, becoming the stonemason's yard and storage area. The total cost of the work was £104,000.

Part of the charm of Llangollen Bridge lies in its irregular arches, their span being governed by the rock structure of the riverbed. From earliest times the Bridge was described as being one of the 'Tri' Thlws Cymru' — the 'Three Jewels of Wales'. The aspect commanded from this historic structure is equal in beauty.

Leaving the railway end of the Bridge and turning left we immediately reach the point at which a tollgate once stood, as shown clearly on page 44.

If one is able to look closely at the original painting (from the author's own collection), it will be noticed that a man on horseback can be faintly seen passing through the gateway. Pencilled in, but not painted — the artist obviously forgot! The buildings to the right of the painting exist today but are a little altered. In the centre the low building with two bow windows remains relatively unchanged, as does its neighbour to the left. To the right, with external staircase, was the Pen y Bont Inn now with a new façade and extra top storey and now known by its English and grander title of the Bridgend Hotel. Across the road are to be seen the steps running down to the river, giving access to the public watering place — an ancient right. No railway yet. The river appears calm as a millpond, which must be taken as artistic licence!

Behind the tollgate cottage lay the village green, surrounded in those days by a suprising number of houses as is shown in the companion picture by the same artist.

Llangollen Bridge before the railway. From an original watercolour in the author's collection (artist unknown).

It is possible that only one of these remains, allowing for the painter's somewhat unreliable perspective. The rest were swept away to accommodate the railway. The large building to the right is Llangollen Mill and crossing the bridge is a mail coach drawn by two — rather deformed — horses.

In the area of the former Village Green, several place names remain to remind us of its presence — *Green* Lane, *Green* Lodge and *Green* Villa. The Green was used for recreations such as sports, dancing, and so on, and belonged to the townspeople. On it was held the *Gorsedd* to proclaim the 1858 Eisteddfod. When it was acquired by the Railway Company a new Green had to be purchased in the form of a piece of land now part of the playing fields of Dinas Brân School and known locally as 'The Rec'. Being somewhat divorced from the town, this has never enjoyed the same amount of use or popularity of the old Green, but it is important to remember that this is part of the heritage of Llangollen and as such must be closely guarded.

Returning to the other end of the Bridge it is as well to stop a while and consider the original layout of Llangollen. Looking directly ahead, up what is now Castle Street, would have been open fields (possibly with a rough cart track coming down) which would have stretched away for as far as the eye could see in the direction of Corwen. To the right, Dee Lane would lead down to the Mill, petering out into a footpath along the river. To the left was the real town stretching along Bridge Street to its junction with Chapel Street to the right. One could turn — Hand Inn on one corner, old Post Office on the other — up to the little square before the Armoury. The road to Corwen led off left along Hall Street.

Mail coach crossing Llangollen Bridge. From an original watercolour in the author's collection (artist unknown).

Alternatively, continue along Bridge Street into Church Street and over Pont Felin Hen at the top following the road up Birch Hill and so on in the direction of Froncysyllte. Mr. Telford greatly altered all this in 1815 when, having the manpower and benefit of 'modern' methods, he was able to cut his Holyhead Road by a flatter and more direct route.

In 1897 'Guto nuth Bran' wrote:

"The number of public houses and breweries in our little town is a disgrace to the community. To take a walk from the station through Bridge Street to the end of Church Street and count the number of 'pubs' and try to realise the poverty, misery, and sin, which floods forth from those fountains of corruption is enough to make one's blood boil."

It would be good to follow the same route as in the days of old Llangollen, taking care to avoid temptation and the 'fountains of corruption' — no easy task as there are still a dozen public houses within this little town. Turning left after crossing the Bridge, the first of these is to be found immediately on the left-hand side — The Royal Hotel, previously called 'The King's Head' until the visit of the young Princess Victoria in 1832. The King's Head was an important coaching inn and many famous people alighted here as the old visitor's book shows. One of whom, the Irish patriot, Daniel O'Connel made the following entry:

"I remember this village with very bad cheer
Ere the Lies, God bless them, set this Inn here;
Let him stay at this Inn or go tho that ere.

*But all who can read will sure understand
How vastly superior the Head's to the Hand."*

The painter, William Gavin Herdman must have completed the work very soon after Victoria's visit as in the picture on the next page the building is seen sporting both names. Next door are the premises of the HSBC/Midland Bank, formally the North and South Wales Bank. Also on the right is the 'Woolpack Inn', a name relevant to the time when the economy of the town was based primarily on agriculture. Across the road is the smart black and white façade of the Wynnstay Arms, formerly the Eagles Inn and a leading hostelry, still having all the ambience of more leisurely days. Note the wide stone steps leading to the front door which would have also been used as a mounting block for horsemen.

It will be noticed that from the beginning of Bridge Street to its junction with Chapel Street that almost every building is of a commercial nature. Little has changed in two hundred years except for the nature of the businesses concerned. It was with one of these shopkeepers that George Borrow held his chapter-long conversation in 1854.

Having reached the Chapel Street junction the low, grey, gabled building on the right was the original Post Office — 'Yr Hen Llyddyrdy'. On the eastern wall is a small plaque informing the passer by that this was in fact the old Post Office of coaching days. Beyond the plaque, which covers the actual aperture through which letters could be posted, the original collecting drawer remains intact. In later years this building became the Workingman's Institute housing a library in a long room on the first floor.

On the opposite corner stands the Hand Hotel, one of the principal coaching inns of the town, which takes its name from the red or bloody hand crest of the Myddleton family of Chirk Castle. It will be remembered that, until recent years, this family owned the ruined Castell Dinas Brân. Under earlier private ownership, the Hand held a great reputation for high-class comfort and was much used by the gentry whose servants could be housed in an adjacent building.

In the 1920s servant's rooms were charged at two shillings per day, with board at a standard five shillings. 'All in' terms — two pounds, nine shillings per week. Boarding terms for their lords and masters began at three pounds, ten shillings per week, plus extras, some of which were, private sitting rooms at five shillings per week, with an attendance charge of one shilling & sixpence per person, per day. (This being an historic account allows us not to have to convert to decimal currency!) Fires lit in rooms were charged at one shilling and sixpence per day, or one shilling for the evening.

En suite facilities were, of course, unknown but bathing was possible at a cost. A sponge or hip bath (hot or cold) was charged at sixpence each, or one shilling if taken in a bathroom. Single room supplements were charged even then, at two shillings and sixpence or more.

The Hotel boasted sixty bedrooms and the public rooms included a drawing room, dining room, billiard room, lounge, smoking room and writing room. Motor car accommodation for thirty vehicles, was in a large, corrugated metal, hanger-like building. Not exactly attractive.

Both the Hand and the Royal hotels traditionally employed a harpist to play in their entrance halls. Looking at the photograph it would seem that he was hard put to find room enough for both his instrument and himself. The interior has been much altered since that time.

Opposite the Hotel is the private garden, reserved for guests, which affords a fine view of the river today. In earlier days the Town Hall and Market House occupied this site of which, sadly, there appears to be no pictorial record.

Continuing along into Church Street with the Churchyard wall immediately and appropriately to the right, the first and rather attractive house on the riverside, Bryn Dwr, was for many years the home of a family who, working upon the premises, made their living by the production of hand-forged iron nails. Glancing across the road one is struck by the realisation of how very land-locked the eastern end of the parish Church really

The entrance hall of the Hand Hotel c.1910.

is. The three tall houses with small gardens in front certainly lie within its shadow.

A little past Bryn Dwr there is a gap in the housing, apparently leading down to the river, at the bottom of which one of Llangollen's earliest Nonconformist Chapels once stood, now long forgotten.

Beyond this, disguised as a dwelling house, is the ancient Talbot Inn. So much

Royal Hotel and the river by moonlight. From the painting by W.G. Herdman (in the author's collection).

The Church from Bridge Street in the late 18th century. The Talbot Inn is to the right. By permission of the National Museum of Wales Welsh Folk Museum.

modernised over the years that only the depth of the window reveals gives the clue to its antiquity. An early painting, now in the possession of the National Museum of Wales and lodged at St Fagan's Castle, gives a rather romantic view of this area in what is claimed to be the late 18th century. The Talbot Inn is shown as the lower part of the gabled buildings on the extreme right. One feels the need to allow for a certain degree of artist's licence.

Continuing up Church Street, on the right and in an elevated position, stands an ancient cottage of part timber-framed construction. The massive external stone chimney on the east gable indicates an original open hearth, which would have been used for both heating and cooking. From here up to the major road junction was originally a healthy mix of private houses and shop premises. In recent years many shop fronts, which had remained intact even after the particular business behind had given way to domestic dwelling, have fallen victim to replacement windows, sometimes of unsuitable design. Windows are the eyes of the house — should they be badly proportioned or positioned the entire face may appear disfigured. Many will remember a draper, baker and grocer all continuing old, established businesses in upper Church Street in comparatively recent years.

Also in this area are one or two surviving decorative fanlights of Georgian design, and one house even has a fire insurance company's plaque on the upper storey. In former times this was erected to indicate that the premises were in fact insured, thus making it worth the while of the local Fire Brigade to attend in the event of a conflagration.

Probably the most striking building in this area is the fancy dress 'Tudorbethan' timbered, gabled and leaded-glass, black and white building on the left, for many years used as offices for the Llangollen Tanning Company, whose extensive and odorous premises lay behind it on the river bank. It is said the original builder was a newly rich Victorian businessman who wished to rival Plas Newydd in the splendour of his dwelling. His efforts are certainly worthy of note.

Down an alley to the left, now the entrance to a new housing development, stood Benjamin Square, built as housing for employee's of the cotton mill which stood here before the tannery. The square can be seen in the watercolour on page 49, immediately down the river from the Bridge and weir, slightly right of centre.

The late Miss Olive Langford told how she had lived as a child in one of these houses and vividly remembered how the entire fabric of the building would shudder and vibrate when the great factory engine was started up. She also remembered the last building on the left, yet another inn at that time, being run as a common lodging house known as 'Slawson's'. It seems that every year a Russian would appear accompanied by

An early 19th century watercolour showing Llangollen from Pen y Coed (in the author's collection).

a rather aged performing bear with which he would beg about the streets of Llangollen. It was his custom to put up for the night as Slawson's, much to the excitement of local children anxious for a sighting of the bear. A commonly-held belief was that bear and master slept together for warmth in the coldest of weather!

The *Llangollen Advertiser* for the 29th November 1895 reported that George Slawson of Church Street had been charged with the offence of depositing filth on the highway, for which he was fined five shillings plus costs. Perhaps the bear had been staying there!

Slawson's is easily identified being almost in the centre of the picture with a wide gable-end chimney. Over to the left, the very tall, smoking, chimney belonged to Llangollen gasworks — now gone, but known to have been established as early as 1853.

We have now completed our stroll along Church Street and reached Pont Felin Hen, Old Mill Bridge — indicating that in early days Pengwern Watermill existed above this spot. The little rushing river Cyflymen (Swift) in much haste to join the River Dee was power enough to turn a mill wheel.

Across the way the large, grey, stone building on the road side to the right, began life as the Sun Brewery, founded by a Mr. Baker whose large residence, Plas yn Llan, stood behind the trees a little further on. The house has been renamed in recent years. Across the road stands the Sun Inn where Baker's Ales were retailed. The Sun Brewery also occupied premises at the rear of No. 28 and 32 Regent Street, opposite the Church, which would have predated the Plas yn Llan buildings. Said premises later became the Cadno Café.

With the decline of brewing, as motoring became more fashionable, the Sun Brewery became the Sun Garage. This enterprise was run successfully for many years by two generations of the Edwards family. Now the premises have yet another use and the petrol pumps, which stood perilously close to the road, are gone and almost forgotten.

A little lane running up from the left, provides the pedestrian with a short, steep climb to Plas Newydd (of which more later) — worth taking for a short way in order to view the curious corner building known locally as 'The Shack'. This property served during its long life both as a Chapel and as a brewery, and now seems to have settled into graceful old age as a residence of character.

It was in this small brewery that ale was brewed for the Talbot Inn. During this period a man named Davies who lived in Factory (Benjamin) Square was drowned in the vat. Having overslept and being late for work at 6 a.m., he had in his haste forgotten to put his stockings on and meeting an acquaintance on the road, had shown a bare leg with the comment 'Mae Sane Iesu Grist Geni heddw'. A rough translation is 'my stockings today are what God gave me'! Soon afterwards he fell into the vat and was drowned.

Min y Dwr, the attractive adjacent house, facing onto the Cyflymen, had a dog spit in the kitchen. Not, of course, to be confused with an ill-mannered canine, but a small treadmill set into the thickness of the fireplace wall, which after having the little dog placed in position would, by a system of rope and pulley, rotate the roasting spit before the fire. It was always said that the dog enjoyed its treadmill, but is not certain that anyone really asked him. We do hope he was suitably rewarded.

Returning to the main road, it is important to remember that in early Llangollen the busy thoroughfare into the town was but a rough footpath. So, we follow the road over the bridge, turning right to enter an area once quite densely populated. The green, grassy bank to the left held a stepped terrace of charming little houses, swept away at the time of building the new fire station in order to allow easier access for the large engines.

Beyond stands Penllyn Chapel built in 1840 as the British School which once housed as many as 222 pupils and is forever linked with the favourite story of Mary and her little lamb.

The wide approach to Horseshoe Pass View was once the site of Pengwern Square — a courtyard of tall, grey houses and a dog-legged straggle of terraced and other cottages, leading up to Pen y Coed — all demolished some thirty-five years ago. Over the way, the group of houses leading down to the Cyflymen was known as the 'City' — a close-knit community where many large families were raised.

At the top of the road, before the coming of the housing estate, the gate guarding the entrance to Pengwern Hall estate barred further progress. A lodge cottage housed a wheel in the front parlour, vertically mounted as on the bridge of a ship, which when turned would open or close the entrance gate. This was a great convenience to the gatekeeper, particularly in foul weather. Having not been invited to visit Plas Pengwern, we must return to the main thoroughfare.

Venturing a little way in the direction of Froncysyllte, mention must be made of the attractive little tollgate cottage abutting the road. Here, legend states, Mary deposited the famous lamb which followed her to school from her Llangollen Fechan home. For years, a large plaster model of a spring lamb supplied by a local butcher gazed dolefully through a front window.

Next door is Walton House, once a private school and now divided into houses. The first floor balcony has a fine decorative railing worthy of note. From here the coach-road takes a steep route up Birch Hill and again past Bryn Dethol on its way to the border but we must quickly retrace our steps to Chapel Street for there is still much to see.

Back to the Hand Inn and round the corner into Chapel Street with nothing of interest until we reach the entrance into the Hand Yard and through it an entrance to the parish Church. The characterless building on the facing corner marks the site of the ancient Royal Oak Inn, sadly demolished to allow the erection of purpose-built staff accommodation for the Hand Hotel.

Opposite stood Rowlands' Grocery Store and dwelling house of which only the shop end remains, the rest having being pulled down to make way for the later, weighty, redbrick premises of E. Evans, Grocer, now an antique shop.

Rowlands Grocery Store with the proprietor standing before the left-hand window.

And so, passing yet another fountain of corruption, the Cross-Foxes Inn, the Town Square is eventually reached. Vicarage to the left, County Hall and Armoury building to the right, and a long row of mainly terraced dwelling houses opposite leading into Hall Street (also known as *Pentre Morgan*). Greenbank, the large bay windowed Victorian villa, facing onto the square was built in front of, and incorporated, a much earlier house. Others gave way to the building of imposing Rehobeth Chapel, the one remaining to cling helplessly onto the right-hand side-wall like an orphaned child, served as schoolroom and vestry.

Where the car parking area is found today once stood a stepped terrace, including a tall, cut Cefn sandstone building built as a brewery but later becoming yet another inn, The Ship, with cavern-like brick barrel vaults built in to the hillside. One of these contained a deep and beautifully constructed well of the purest water. A smaller house in the adjacent terrace was again the home of a family of nailers as advertised by the plaque on the front wall, fashioned in the form of an anvil, dated 1844 and bearing the initials *J & ST*. At the time of the demolition of these properties, the plaque was salvaged and set into the gable end of the house known as the Willows, a little further on.

Continuing along Hall Street and keeping to the left, the roofline is broken by the solid, three-storey building known as the Glyn. Here a previous acquaintance reappears, Rondle Reade, in the form of his master mason's stone, discovered during the 1873 widening of the bridge. Just how he came to be embedded here is a matter of mystery, which serves to deceive those unaware of his antecedents. This building was a tannery for many years.

Before leaving Hall Street, a little enclave of cottages can be seen. This is known as Bala Bach and once contained a smithy. It was from one of these houses that the unfortunate John Thomas, a twenty-six year old collier, stole a shirt — probably from the washing line — in January 1897. Alas, he was apprehended and made to pay dearly for his crime, being sentenced to six months hard labour. We hope the shirt was worth it.

Continuing along in the direction of Berwyn is the large roadside building that began life as Tanquery's Brewery, the Brewmaster living high above in a now demolished house known as Pen y Bryn. Let this be an appropriate point to leave the highway,

E. Edwards, Ty Issa Dairy, with prize-winning horse and float at Bala Bach, Hall Street.

taking a footpath through the fields to the riverbank thence townwards to Llangollen Mill.

The original watermill on this site was built by the Cistercian monks from Valle Crucis Abbey and was largely rebuilt in the 18th century. It continuously ground flour for over six hundred years, its prominent position becoming a local landmark.

Continuing up Dee Lane with the Old Smithy building on the right, we emerge at the Bridge — just a little footsore and weary perhaps. A good enough reason for entering one of those inns at last. But not the one on the corner, for that was a Temperance Tavern!

Llangollen in c.1860 showing the building of the Baptist Chapel and some of Castle Street.

Further Developments and the Outlying Districts

Three major 19th century events had a great impact upon the development of Llangollen and its environs. First, Mr. Thomas Telford, having completed his now famous aqueduct, brought his canal through the town and on to Llantysilio where he constructed the Horseshoe Falls to feed, or rather, water it. This work was not completed until 1808 and so the aqueduct must have temporarily received its water from another source, it being opened for traffic in 1805.

In turn, this created exciting new possibilities for Llangollen, providing a cheap and reliable form of transport to improve the economy of the town. Coal came in from the North Wales coalfield and pottery which had previously been brought by journeymen with donkeys with panniers, arrived from Buckley and Staffordshire. Imported bricks and other building materials, changed the appearance of new properties which had previously been constructed from the materials immediately to hand — mostly locally quarried freestone.

Grander properties where constructed, wholly or in part, from dressed sandstone from the Cefn Mawr quarries. There were few such buildings in Llangollen.

Exports included slate and slate products, limestone and agricultural lime from the many kilns in the Llangollen area, some arable produce including flour and, of course, casks of ale. The Canal also speeded the industrial development of the town, turning

Pentrefelin Wharf with the little petrol station just visible above the barge.

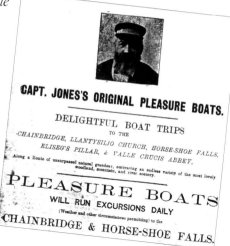

cottage industries into major places of employ-ment. It is easy to forget that the canals were intended to be commercial waterways without any thought given to tourist or holiday traffic. The latter have now become the prime users and as one watches boatload after boatload of mums, dads, dogs and children chugging along in peak season, would hardly credit the British transport commissioners decision in the 1950s to abandon and close down the Llangollen Canal. However, this threat was strenuously opposed and the commissioners changed their minds. This waterway now also serves to supply good Welsh water to parts of Cheshire which can only lead to the betterment of their health!

Pleasure boats on the Llangollen Canal were a great feature of Victorian and Edwardian times, as commercial traffic was transferred to the railways and much-improved road networks. The original trading wharf above the town made the ideal base for the new pleasure boats and the little white cottage on Wharf Hill made the perfect residence for the proprietor, the wife of one of whom was famous for her invitation issued to long unseen acquaintances:

"We live by the canal — when you're passing, drop in."

As indeed one could — from their very back yard.

The heavily-bearded Captain Jones, as his advertisement informs, was the originator of this delight. Rather confusingly, he ran eleven trips per day to the Horseshoe Falls but, curiously, only advertised eight return journeys. The explanation may be that, at certain times, two boats would return together rather than having to allow for the possibility of three sinking on the outward journey!

The single fare was threepence, sixpence there and back. From Whit Sunday and on each successive Sabbath during the season, a special Churchgoers boat left Llangollen at 2.30 p.m. for those wishing to attend the English service held at Llantysilio Church at 3.15 p.m.. The boats were, of course, horse-drawn and journey took roughly half an hour. Captain Jones also had rowing boats for hire, but rowers were expected to strike off in the Trevor direction for fear of meeting a pleasure boat and getting into difficulties. Pleasure boats are still to be found running from the same wharf. Captain Jones and his rowing boats are now long gone.

The second major development was also undertaken by the great Thomas Telford — his Holyhead road. This he began in 1815, its construction taking in all some fifteen years of which the Welsh section proved to be the most difficult. The Llangollen stretch was one of the last to be completed, work to the west having been done first. Bwlch y Rhysgog proved to be a very difficult area and necessitated a severe bend, which became an accident 'blackspot' for later, faster motor traffic.

The new stretch of flat road from Bryn Dethol, through Llangollen Fechan to Pont Felin Hen, thereafter following the old footpath route along what is now Regent Street, continuing out in the direction of Berwyn, provided a much easier approach to Llangollen. Property development followed and it will be appreciated that with two such major works taking place, canal and road, the early years of the 19th century saw considerable immigration into the town.

And then came the railway. The first passenger train arrived at the Old Vicarage Terminus on the 2nd June 1862, preceded by the first goods train which made history by chugging along the valley in December 1861 — to the great consternation of the local sheep and cows.

Before this time, the nearest railway station had been at Whitehurst, officially called Llangollen Road Station but known within the town as 'Stesion Ty Coch'. Coaches and other local conveyances made regular daily trips to meet the trains, all the major inns having vehicles of their own employed for this purpose. A popular romantic novel published some two or three years ago makes mention of the heroine taking the mail coach 'Defiance' after having alighted from the railway train at Llangollen Road Station. The coach at least was not a figment of the author's imagination, for a coach called 'Defiance' did indeed make a daily run from Dolgellau to Whitehurst, calling at the King's Head Inn, Llangollen to refresh both horses and passengers. Although trains still run through Whitehurst they no longer stop and the station building is now a private residence.

Let it not be imagined that the first train arrived at Llangollen terminus without much prior discourse — and disagreement. First, it had to be decided from which point upon the main line the Llangollen branch line would leave. Many favoured the Chirk–Whitehurst stretch, which would then have brought the new line to the town along the south side of the valley. This route would have inevitably benefited the quite extensive limeworks at Froncysyllte and was, of course, opposed by the owners of the Sun Bank quarries. The latter also held the argument that, by taking the north side route, much revenue would be raised from goods traffic from the ironworks at Acrefair and the coal mines both there and at Trefynant.

The *Wrexham Advertiser* for 23rd October 1858 gave a full account of the meeting held in the County Hall, Llangollen on 16th October, the purpose of which was to decide both the desirability of bringing a railway to Llangollen and the route it should take. Among those present were many of the great and the good of the area. The townsfolk were represented by such as Major Tottenham, Plas Rhysgog; Mr. Richard Ellerton, Braich y Gwynt (later called Bryntysilio); the Reverend William Edwards, Vicar; Dr John Pritchard, Baptist Minister; Charles Richards, Banker and Solicitor; Mr. James Clark, Schoolmaster and Mr. William Morgan (Pentre Morgan), Brewer and prominent Methodist.

Colonel R.M. Biddulph of Chirk Castle was elected to be chairman and the meeting was a long one. First, it was carried:

"That the line construction of a Railway to Llangollen would be a great public advantage and is deserving of the support of the town and neighbourhood."

The chairman then presented what he considered to be two very pertinent recommendations, which were:

"That the line constructed should be one that would bring the greatest benefit to the town."

"That the branch should join the main line at the nearest possible point, so that the line constructed should be the shortest possible."

Both were eminently sensible. Rather more so than one suggestion, which would have seen the railway terminating in a field above the house known as 'Siamber Wen'. One imagines the steep gradient would have been far too much for the pulling power of the small locomotives of those days, as Sun Bank was to almost prove to be.

Let us now be far less long-winded than the meetings proved and précis the outcome. A company was set up, the 'Vale of Llangollen Railway Company', with the object of constructing a railway from, initially, Ruabon to Llangollen and terminating upon Vicarage Field. Henry Robertson of the New British Ironworks, Acrefair, was appointed Chief Engineer. He estimated the cost of construction to be £9,000 per mile — a great sum of money for those days — and the company was set up with a capital of £45,000 in shares of £5 each. Robertson and his friends were willing to advance £5,000 each. Principle Llangollen shareholders included Watkin Richards, Major Tottenham of Plas Rhysgog, Ebeneser Cooper, Alex Reid, Llantysilio and Dr. Robertson of Siamber Wen.

The contractors were Brassey and Field, Thomas Brassey being a close friend of William Wagstaff of Plas yn Vivod who, by the marriage of his daughter Mary to Captain John Charles Best, RN established the dynasty of Best of Vivod. The elaborate wooden porte cochere at Plas yn Vivod was a gift to Wagstaff from Brassey, having been made in his railway works in Cheshire.

The contractors promised completion by May 1861 but it was a little overtime regardless of a 'great number of navvies and masons' being employed. There was criticism from the *Llangollen Advertiser*, who deplored seeing so many young men working on Sundays:

"For our part rather than the Lord's Day be profaned, let the opening of the line be delayed a few weeks."

As indeed it proved to be. Incredibly wet weather, frost and snow, more than once brought the work to a standstill. The first train — goods only — arrived without pomp or ceremony. However, hundreds of people crowded the Vicarage Field to await the arrival of the first passenger train. History does not relate how many passengers actually alighted and what their impressions really were of such a momentous journey.

What is recorded, however, is that one year before the first train actually arrived 'The Llangollen and Corwen Railway Company' had been set up with the intention of extending the railway as far as Corwen. The list of directors and shareholders reads pretty much as last, with Mr. Charles Richards having being appointed Secretary at a salary of £100 per annum.

Work began, rather tentatively, in March 1861 but the business of actually continuing the line through this northern end of the town was thwarted by difficulties, which were not only of a physical nature.

First, the townsfolk's ancient right to take water from the river for washing purposes would be lost — the railway line cut through the steps giving access to the riverbank. Also, the old hand pump known as 'Pistill Penybont', which supplied drinking water, stood squarely in the path of progress and would have to go. It must be remembered that few homes at this time enjoyed the benefit of piped water.

Then there was the problem of the Bridge itself. It would be necessary to cut through the northern end in order to allow the line to pass through. Both problems were eventually overcome in 1863 after protracted negotiations with the Llangollen Board of Health. The Railway Company replaced the existing pump with two new ones — supplying fresh water from one, washing water only from the other. The condition applied to cutting through the Bridge allowed for a high wall of matching stone to be erected between the railway and the road with a similarly constructed retaining wall rising from the river. This work was completed as directed, the ornamental tower being built at the same time.

Then followed the vexed problem of the Village Green and the houses about it plus the sixty or so *Penddol* dwellings, mostly the homes of local weavers. Curiously, Henry Robertson himself had purchased these some little time before! The Green was protected by an Act of Parliament, which allowed for its free use for recreational purposes and there were many opposed to the possible loss of this. Again, very protracted negotiations took place and even though the Llangollen Board of Health had been persuaded to sell the Green to the Railway Company in 1861 for £150, it was ten years before the matter was resolved by returning the purchase price in exchange for an acre of land of similar size. As a result we have the present recreation ground adjacent, but not belonging to, Dinas Brân School.

The old Tollgate Cottage was demolished at the same time as the sixty *Penddol* dwellings, the now valuable property of Henry Robertson. The late Charles Roberts of Ty Ddu was brought up in one of the latter. He clearly remembered that, after the demolition of their home, he and his family were accommodated in the Coach House of the Pen y Bont Inn until the new houses to become known as Princess Street were built.

And so, all local obstacles having been removed, the railway continued in the direction of Corwen. Once again, the Chief Engineer was Henry Robertson and the Chief Surveyor was Henry Smyth of Coventry, a very talented artist, who in his leisure moments painted several fine views of the district. One of these, a large oil of 'Llangollen from the Geraint' was purchased for the town in the 1970s and is hanging in the library at Plas Newydd.

The railway reached Corwen in May 1865, the Berwyn Tunnel having taken a year to complete and at the cost of one life. This work was done with two gangs of navvies, one at each end, cutting through the rock and hoping to meet about the middle. Their objective was achieved with much difficulty. Experts used to claim that they could feel a slight bump as their train crossed the point at which both ends met. The railwayman's version

An early train coming through the newly-cut railway arch.

of the *Princess and the Pea*, perhaps.

Berwyn Station is both attractive and picturesquely situated, looking across the rushing River Dee to the Velvet Mountain. It owes its existence to Major Tottenham who made it a condition in allowing the railway to cross his land that a station should be built for his use and benefit. He was of course also a shareholder, which helped!

And so, with the arrival of the London to Holyhead trunk road, the canal and completion of the railway, Llangollen was well and truly on the map. It was therefore inevitable that the town should develop to accommodate such changing times. Logic dictated that the shortest route should link the Bridge and Mr. Telford's new road in order to avoid the winding and narrow Bridge Street–Church Street progression.

In 1853 there was a severe epidemic of Smallpox and Scarlet Fever raging in Llangollen, and a petition was sent from the parish to the General Board of Health in Trafalgar Square in London to ask for an inquiry; the Public Health Act having been passed in 1848. The report of this enquiry gives conditions of community life at the time. Public sanitation, of course, was non-existent. Llangollen was no worse than other towns, for Wrexham reports of about the same year describe similar conditions. The green fields, which stretched from the Armoury to the Mill, carried accumulations of filth and the rest was swept into the river by a couple of the small streams which ran freely through the town. However, it is interesting to note that the Gas Company was already in existence and that they were contracting for twenty-four public lights. It was due to this inquiry that a local Board of Health was set up in Llangollen and its bylaws were authorised at Whitehall on the 18th July 1857.

After this, development was rapid and Castle Street, as we know it, was built to provide the needed direct route from the Holyhead Road to the Bridge. The built up area to the west of it followed on during 1860s and 70s, being planned more as a whole than the piece-meal development of the old town. This can be seen from the grid-like arrangement of streets which made it possible for the first time 'to take a walk around the block' for those of a mind to do so.

One or two older buildings managed to survive, however. An example being the old foundry still standing between the houses in Market Street and those in Princess Street; so hemmed in that one would not be aware of its existence. Mercifully for the neighbours, this building is no longer occupied by a noisy foundry but is the workshop of a local carpenter who plies his trade in quiet and considerate manner.

Much of the 'West End' development was seen as an opportunity for speculative investment by local people among whom were the Roberts family of Ashgrove and the Rogers family whose butchers and greengrocers' shops

LOT 3.

ALL THAT FREEHOLD RESIDENCE, known as OSBORNE HOUSE, situate in PRINCESS STREET and WEST STREET (having a frontage in the former Street of 64 feet, and in the latter of 51 feet), containing spacious tiled Entrance Halls, 3 Reception Rooms, 4 Bedrooms, 3 good Attics, 2 Bath Rooms and W.Cs., Front and Back Staircases, Large Kitchen, Back Kitchen, Wash-house, Cellar, Yard, and Offices.

This House is extremely well built and in good repair, and thoroughly finished throughout, with a front and back entrance in Princess Street, and a front entrance in West Street, and has an ornamental wall, iron railing and garden in front.

Having a commanding elevation, it stands in one of the most charming situations, embracing an unsurpassed view of the surrounding Mountain and River Scenery, and is extremely suitable for a Private Residence or Lodging House, being within 3 minutes' walk of the Railway Station and the centre of the Town. All the rooms are well arranged, lofty and very commodious. Now in the occupation of Mrs. Roberts.

An extract from particulars of sale by auction at the Eagles Hotel, 1st May 1888.

were so long a feature of Market Street. These houses were brick built — an innovation, as the old town was built of random, local stone. It will be noticed that many of the faces of the properties looking across to the Smithfield are ornamented with locally-made decorative cast iron lintels.

By 1888, the first of the Princess Street houses had been standing long enough for the original speculators to feel that it was time to realise their investment — hopefully at a profit. Numbers 1 to 11 were sold by auction at the Eagles Hotel at three of the clock, on Tuesday 1st May. Offered in two lots, numbers 1, 3, and 5 "well built and in good repair contain: Kitchen (each kitchen being fitted with a large cupboard), back Kitchen, 2 Bedrooms, brick yard and WC; producing a gross annual rental of £24-15s" were sold to Edward Davies for £420. Lot 2, Nos. 7, 9 and 11 "in capital repair" and similar to Lot 1 but also having "Attic & Offices", was sold to Mrs. Rogers for £350, their gross annual rental being only £22-10s.

It was of course inevitable that the wide new street from Telford's road to the Bridge should become the principal trading area. Tall new buildings housing grander shops than Llangollen had ever known before proudly lined both sides of the thoroughfare, together with two impressive Chapels. A distinguished Town and Market Hall was erected in 1867 by Lloyd Williams & Underwood upon a prominent corner site, with a grand colonnade of open arches giving access to a covered market area at ground level. It is perhaps a matter of some regret that this feature lasted but a few short years — the space was later subdivided into retail shops, etc.

Around the corner into Parade Street a formidable police station and courtroom by the same architects was erected about the same time. Tucked discreetly away was a mortuary — which few had any real desire to enter. The Post Office moved into the premises now occupied by Barclays' Bank, although this was not to be its permanent home. It will

A view of the newly-built Castle Street, c.1868.

be noticed that most of the Castle Street buildings are three storeys high, which allowed for not only the proprietors and their families to live above but also rooms at the top of the house to accommodate a maid and a shop assistant or two. The late Mrs. Cuffin, Glancollen, remembered a small errand boy sleeping under the counter in her stepfather's shop. Assistants often came from country districts and long hours plus lack of transport made it difficult for them to get home.

Many of the premises sported façades which strived to display grandeur and use was made of the new high-fired glazed red brick made by J.C. Edwards at Ruabon, and Pen y Bont Brickworks. This brick was also employed in building the grand new houses along Abbey Road. Terracotta ornamental decoration was much in fashion. One really needs to look up in order to observe many of these features — not advisable when crossing the road.

The growth of Nonconformism was responsible for the building of many substantial places of worship about the town, each proudly attempting to outshine its competitors in architectural style. Regardless of their influence, the 1890s were obviously thirsty years because it was possible to visit twenty-five public houses — if one had the stamina. About half of these would be unknown names to most of the townsfolk of today, examples being the *Crow Castle Inn, Queen Inn, Waterloo Inn, Butcher's Arms, Red Lion, Golden Lion Vaults, Forester's Vaults, White Lion, Ship Inn* and *Dee Tavern*, all of which have run dry many moons since. The last of them was the *Waterloo*.

In 1897 there was a plan to establish a large area of housing at the top of Hill Street on land previously belonging to the Plas Newydd Estate. A total of twenty-five plots, each with an average frontage of thirty-three feet but of varying depth, were offered for sale by public auction on 12th April at three in the afternoon at the Eagles Hotel. The layout allowed for the provision of two new service roads and the conditions were to impose a restriction in the interest of the purchasers as to the rentals of the residences

The Hermitage in its final death agony. Undergrowth almost obscures the lower floor.

to be erected upon each lot. In the event the development was only partially completed and only one new roadway was built. The other remains as a public footpath running at high level to the left of the Hermitage.

The Hermitage house and land has a history of its own. In 1876 General York, CB, a member of the York family of Erddig from whom he inherited some of their delightful innocent eccentricity, purchased Plas Newydd and its adjacent fields. He remembered the Ladies from his childhood, never forgetting their kindness when he was thrown from his pony whilst attempting to ascend Dinas Brân. They had attended to his bruises and injured pride with soothing words and a gift of oranges.

Unlike the Ladies, of whom it was rumoured that they had never spent a night away from their beloved home, General Yorke chose never to spend a night in his, choosing instead to visit daily from his base camp at the Hand Hotel. In the greatly extended residence, he set up a quaint collection devoted in part to the Ladies, the rest becoming a museum of esoteric objects, which was open to the public. The items displayed were numerous and included the skeletal head of a sea serpent as well as a china model of Madame Vestris' leg!

He was also moved to build a large detached 'gothic' villa to be called 'The Hermitage' on land to the north west of Plas Newydd. The two properties were separated from each other by a narrow lane but united via an underground tunnel, which burrowed beneath it. As far as is known, the General spent not a night in the new house either, which remained part of the Plas Newydd property until Llangollen Urban District Council acquired the whole in 1932.

For the last years of its life, Mr. & Mrs. Albert Davies occupied the Hermitage as the caretaker's residence. It was a curious, gabled house rising to three floors, built of cut Cefn sandstone with long 'gothic' windows, the panes of which were leaded in a diamond pattern. Inside, a rather spitefully steep staircase attempted to fling the descender into the not over-large entrance hall from which led off two long but badly proportioned reception rooms. They were too narrow for their length, terminating in tall bay windows, which somehow emphasised the unwarrantedly lofty ceiling height. A passage led off to the nether regions, which mercifully included a comfortable kitchen, quite the best room in the house.

Above, the bedrooms followed the same pattern as the rooms below, there being one bathroom of ungenerous proportions. It was, in fact, so cramped that it was necessary to place the washbasin above the bath into which it happily emptied when the plug was removed. All this architectural economy was quite unnecessary, for the Hermitage stood upon a large area of land.

So large, in fact, as to persuade the Town Council in their wisdom that it made sense to demolish the house and cover the site with nice little bungalows. The townspeople rose in wrath and on the evening of Wednesday 30th December 1964 a public meeting was held in the Memorial Hall, which proved to be too small for the great number of people wishing to attend. The meeting was called by the Hermitage Site Petitioners' Committee and was chaired by Mr. D.B. Clay-Jones, later to become a 'household name' famous on both radio and television for his very popular gardening programmes.

The official notice invited:

> *"Both Petitioners and non petitioners to the above meeting which will be*
> *their final opportunity of saving for posterity a little piece of Llangollen*
> *which for decades has been theirs.*
> *WE BEG YOU TO ATTEND THIS MEETING AND EXPRESS YOUR OWN VIEWS."*

Views were indeed most forcibly and fully expressed and a weighty petition presented to the council who replied in the following terms:

> *"The Council welcomed the Petition and the deputation's submission in so far as*
> *they represented a healthy and active interest in a matter of public concern. They*
> *appreciated too the courteous and responsible manner in which their effort was*
> *conducted. Nevertheless taking into account all the circumstances and being*
> *motivated only by what they consider to be best in the broad interests of the town,*
> *they have decided unanimously to re-affirm their intention that the land shall be*
> *devoted to housing purposes."*

And so that was that. The Hermitage came down and the houses went up. Now only the name remains to remind us of the old house.

Previously, Local Authority housing had been developed in three distinct pockets. Two small ones at Park Avenue and Coed Afon with the much larger Pengwern estate being established after the Second World War. It must be remembered that it was not until 1959/60 that Llangollen was to enjoy the benefits of a mains sewage system. Prior to this when plug was removed and chain pulled, all eventually found its way down to the river (where the salmon were fat and plentiful). This was not seen as pollution but just the way things were, if indeed it was considered at all. Locals knew the spots to avoid when walking the rocks during periods of low water. However, public health officials

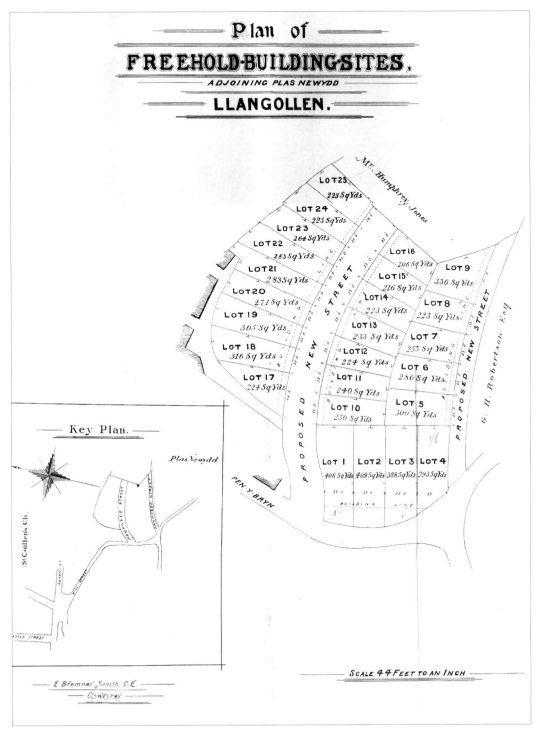

Plan showing a proposed but uncompleted development on Plas Newydd land, April 1897.

Laying new sewage pipes in Castle Street, 1960.

were not so relaxed in their thinking, nor were the planners happy to see new housing erected until something was done.

And done it was — to the great disruption of everyday life in the town. There was also much putting of coloured dye down lavatories followed by rushing about in the hope of discovering where it might emerge. Very often it didn't and there must still be several houses in the old town who cannot for certain say that they are 'on the mains'!

The village of Pentredwr, nestling below the Horseshoe Pass, largely died for lack of 'mains' — mains water in particular. On the main route to Ruthin, before the new road was cut, it was a thriving, self-contained community with school, shop, Post Office and three public houses. There is, sadly, very little to be found today except the Britannia Inn, just before the turning into the village proper, where we find but a few scattered dwellings and farms. The main village street is scarred by a long

The original Britannia Inn in more leisurely days.

footage of derelict land beyond the school and the 1844 Methodist Chapel, both of which have been converted to other uses. On this sight stood a row of stone cottages which also embraced the Post Office (ably kept by Mrs. Elsa Edwards until c.1974) and the Cross-Keys Inn (later to become a house — the last inhabited dwelling).

Beyond were the second Chapel, Bethesda (built 1822, enlarged in 1864 and refurbished 1903) and the shop, which closed in September 1970 at great loss to the community. Mrs. Marion Twardowski, born and bred in Pentredwr, had taken over the running of the business from her parents (the late Edward and Mary Jones). As a family they had kept the shop for seventy-five years. Across the road stands the Old White Hart Inn, now a private dwelling house.

Largely developed at the time of the flourishing slate quarrying industry, much evidence of which is to be seen in the area, Pentredwr also has several earlier dwellings. Included among these are Plas Ddu and Penyclawdd, hospitably farmed by the Evans family for many years, where a stone dated 1631 is to be seen in one of the bedrooms.

Mains water arrived one year too late to save much of the village.

A narrow, scenic roadway leads from the lower village to the hamlet of Eglwyseg where the little Church, built to be both a school and place of worship, is now converted to a dwelling house. Below it, the house known as Ty Newydd served for many years as the local Post Office.

Taking the road back towards Plas Eglwyseg, one passes the entrance to a hidden watermill, long since fallen in to disuse. Past Plas Eglwyseg and on the way to World's End where one can see the fragmented remains of the former Nonconformist Chapel and schoolroom. Eglwyseg has always traditionally been a farming community but also had a short period of prosperity based upon the Pant Glas Slate Quarry, situated high above the road in a wild and exposed position.

An alternative route to Pentredwr follows the narrow lane to the left of the Church,

The lower village, Pentredwr, soon after 1900.

passing through the yard of Tan y Fron Farm and descending steeply downhill to the village. Turning left one is soon back to the Britannia Inn, almost unrecognisable now as the 15th century hostelry it once was. Close by stood one or two roadside cottages, later demolished after being severely damaged by a runaway motor coach whose brakes had failed while descending from the Horseshoe Pass, occasioning some loss of life.

Below the Britannia Inn a narrow road leads off to the right and continues to the twin villages of Llantysilio and Rhewl. These are both estate villages based upon a rural economy and largely owned by the Llantysilio estate family although the mansion house is sadly no longer in their ownership. At Rhewl, the Conquering Hero Inn has, heroically, been converted into a Community Centre at the commendable instigation of the local people. The ancient Sun Inn still remains — happily — and retains many of its original features. Both shop and Post Office are, alas, no longer.

Hebron Chapel was opened in 1904 although there had been a Chapel here since 1826. Methodism in Rhewl has a history going back as early as 1806, worship having originally taken place in private houses.

The parish Church is situated below Llantysilio Hall and is of ancient foundation. There can be few more beautifully situated places of worship within the British Isles. The poet Browning worshipped here when visiting nearby Bryntysilio. A plaque to this effect to be found inside the Church will confirm this. This memorial was set up at the behest of Lady Martin after his death in December 1889. Lady Martin recorded in her journal on 21st September 1890:

"Saw the memorial to dear Robert Browning for the first time. It is put up just by

Llantysilio church before the Victorian restoration.

The interior of Llantysilio Church before the alteration and the fitting of a reredos, which now obscures the lower panes and the dedication on the fine east window.

the side of our pew and close to where he and his sister always sat on my right hand. I had a curious feeling that he was beside me and my attention was taken off the service."

The plaque records that Robert Browning worshipped here for ten weeks in the autumn of 1886. It says a great deal for the charm of Llantysilio Church that Browning, not by any means a regular Churchgoer, should have attended here for ten consecutive weeks.

The Churchyard contains many interesting tombs including that of Exuperius Pickering who built the first Chain Bridge in conjunction with Thomas Telford as, it is said, a prototype for his Menai suspension bridge. Pickering was also involved in the building of Telford's aqueduct at Pontcysyllte.

Llantysilio Hall, the second house to be built here, stands on a more elevated site than its predecessor and would have been approached from the old driveway just a little above the Churchyard entrance. Long since demolished, the house below Tyn Llan — itself an ancient and interesting property — was the birthplace of Deborah Jones, who remembered the demolition of the old Hall in 1875, the new one having been completed in 1874. She had in her possession a teapot stand, made from an octagonal tile encased in wood, the tile having come from the old Hall as did an old tankard of German origin, also in her possession.

Miss Deborah Jones married Rowland Pugh, a Merioneth man and friend of some of the gold miners working at Gwynfynnydd, by whom he was given a "lump of ore —

Fancy dress dance, Llantysilio School, February 1924.

about a hand's width". Rowland Pugh took this to Robert Hughes, the Castle Street jeweller, who was able to extract from it enough gold dust to make Deborah's wedding ring — now buried with her in Llantysilio Churchyard.

Mr. & Mrs. Pugh farmed Pen y Bryn, above the Britannia Inn, and in the ownership of the Llantysilio Hall estate. Here their son, the late Arthur Pugh who continued to farm Pen y Bryn into old age, succeeded them. He gave the tile and tankard referred to earlier to his landlord, Mr. Duncan Robertson, and so a little of the old Hall was admitted to the new after being in the custody of the Pugh family for about one hundred years.

Llantysilio School was built long before that at Pentredwr and it was necessary for the children from that end of the parish to make the journey there on a daily basis. No school buses then of course! Mr. Arthur Pugh remembered the 'shortcut' in regular use was by means of a steep footpath, which passed through Pen y Bryn farmyard. Mrs. Eluned Evans, who recalls her mother telling her about it, has confirmed this.

Out of teaching hours the School, in common with so many others, was the social centre of the village, being used for public meetings, plays, concerts and even wedding receptions.

Bales of flannel from Mile End Mill outside Glanafon in the care of Tom Davies 'the Lorry' and Joe Owens.

Mills and Other Industries

Doubtless the oldest mill in Llangollen is the watermill opposite the railway station, which had ground flour for at least six hundred years. The manufacture of flannel was first carried on in what became the tannery and the business was then moved across the river to Lower Dee Mill — originally a cotton mill — and to Upper Dee Mills. The Mile End Factory was constructed for flannel manufacture. The weaving of wincey and tweed was carried on in small factories such as Ty Brethyn and in cottage homes. Nailers lived at Bryn Dwr, Church Street and in Hall Street as we have already learned.

Llangollen Watermill is prominently situated above the Bridge and is to be seen on many old prints and photographs. It owes its foundation to the Cistercian monks of Valle Crucis and is mentioned in a 13th century document to be found in the London Record Office, dealing with the previously referred to fishing dispute between the freemen of Llangollen and the Abbot of Valle Crucis.

The present mill was rebuilt in 1786 and is for the most part a three-storey building constructed of local stone. The waterwheel is housed inside the building in a separate wheelhouse. Used solely as a corn mill until 1895, it had three pairs of stones for grinding the grain. The family firm of William Jones & Son was founded in 1864 and continued in the old way until 1895, when changing times and conditions necessitated the decision to become a provender mill. Balanced feeds for cattle, pigs and poultry were produced to accommodate the requirements of advanced farming methods.

Staff at Llangollen Mill on the last working day in 1974.

It would seem that the owners had, for a time, a second string — we find the appearance of the following advertisement in the *Llangollen Advertiser*:
"Boy wanted, about 15, to sell milk with horse and trap — Apply Llangollen Mill."

Sadly, the Mill closed in 1974 but remained within the Jones family for a further twenty years or so. During this time it was leased as first the premises of Llangollen Weavers and later an antiques showroom with a small confectioners and a gift shop tacked on at the end. At the time of writing, the premises have new owners and seem destined to become a 'theme pub'. A reminder of the Biblical quotation, here the waters still pass but the mill shall no longer grind.

Lady Eleanor Butler and Miss Ponsonby, who recruited many famous names to their cause, met the arrival of the Industrial Revolution in Llangollen with fierce opposition. Their campaign was brought to the attention of the gossip column writers of several national newspapers to whom they were not unknown. One reported:

"Lady Eleanor Butler and her fair friend Miss Ponsonby, who have for so many years been the fair recluses of the Vale of Llangollen in Wales are going to leave their beautiful seat no longer a retreat from the 'busy hum of men', by two extensive cotton mills having been erected near their abode."

Like so much gossip, this announcement was somewhat exaggerated — the two extensive mills having been restricted to one quite small one by dint of their intervention. The builders, Turner and Comber, came to Llangollen from Manchester in 1805, probably thinking a country district where labour was plentiful and the populace less militant, to be preferable to a city in which their premises could well be at risk from those opposed to modern methods. There was also the great advantage of water power and the canal being constructed close by to provide cheap transport.

Thus, what was to be known as Dee Mills came into operation and, for a time, all went well until a disastrous fire in 1844 which brought production to a halt and hardship to the workers. A local relief fund was set up, encouraged by the Ladies of Plas Newydd who very generously subscribed five guineas each.

Fortunately Turner & Comber had had the foresight to insure their premises with one of the newly established national companies and rebuilding work was able to begin the following year. The new factory occupied a site comprising four acres, thirty-nine perches. The spinning mill building was three storeys high and was powered by an over-shot water wheel twenty-four feet in diameter and five feet wide. It is interesting to note that

Lower Dee Mills and weavers' cottages, c.1969.

the force of water used to drive this wheel was taken from the Canal by means of two large bore cast iron pipes which were still to be seen behind Upper Dee Mills until their removal in 1967.

The weaving mill contained one hundred and forty-three power-looms and was again water powered by two wheels, the water for these being extracted from the River Dee by means of the now destroyed weir which may be seen on many old photographs. Both buildings were heated by steam and lit by gas, which was produced from the mills own

THE "DINAS BRÂN" REAL WELSH SHIRT

Edwardian trade card from Dee Mills — still in use when the business closed!

Charlie Roberts' cottage and pet hen.

plant of three retorts, purifying vessels and a gasometer thirteen-feet in diameter and seventeen feet four inches high.

Also on site were a commodious manager's house with good garden and a further cottage with garden. Sadly, Messrs. Turner & Comber, regardless of their fine new premises and the cheap labour available in Llangollen, did not prosper, being declared bankrupt in April 1819.

The premises were offered for sale by private contract in May of the following year, by Mr. Edwards, solicitor, of Oswestry and eventually purchased by the firm of Gardner, Taylor and Bell who were also a Manchester Company. Sadly, they too met bankruptcy, having borrowed £6,000 in 1829 from Benjamin Parkin, a Cheshire businessman. Six years later only £400 had been repaid plus £198 interest and the company was declared bankrupt. Dee Mill was sold by public auction on 11th May 1835, at the Albion Inn, Chester.

By 1839–40 the Mill had seen a change of ownership and a change of product, from cotton to wool. The new owners Edward Roberts and John Hughes were both natives of the Ceiriog Valley and were initially joined by Thomas Griffiths, also from the same valley, who remained a partner for only a short period of time. It may be that there was something of a clash of temperament between Griffiths and the other two. This was not surprising when one considers that Edward Hughes came to Llangollen in order to become landlord of the Grapes Inn, while Thomas Griffiths was of more puritanical mind and a founder of Penybryn Baptist Chapel above Hill Street.

The Hughes and Roberts partnership seems to have lasted until about 1888. During these years the company prospered, expanding to a site above the Wrexham Road where the Upper Dee Mills were built in 1855. Conditions were reasonably good for the period, work being conducted over a twelve hour day — 6 a.m. to 6 p.m. with two hours in total being allowed for meal breaks. Children were employed from the age of nine years, with an entire family being occasionally employed. Starting pay for a boy was one shilling per week — paid by token — rising to four shillings and sixpence. A man would earn from fifteen to twenty five shillings.

The late Mr. Charlie Roberts, who lived most of his life in a little cottage at the entrance to Lower Dee Mills, had been employed there in 1890 at the age of nine years. Eighty years later one might still call, on a summer's day, to find him sitting in the little porch accompanied by his pet hen. Many were the tales he had to tell.

Upper and Lower Dee Mills did not, of course, have the monopoly over the Llangollen woollen industry. In 1848 Edward Stephen Jones and his partners completed the Mile End Factory alongside the Holyhead Road between Llangollen and Berwyn.

The Roberts family, 10 Dee Mill Place. BACK ROW, LEFT TO RIGHT: Evan, Mary Ann, Elizabeth, Emily, Esther, John Edward (eldest son). FRONT ROW: Joseph (father, Austin, Louisa, Charlie, Rhuama, Selina, Maria (mother). All of the above were employed at Dee Mills at one time or another.

Edward Stephen and his family had come from Corwen to open a draper's shop on Regent Street and were enterprising enough to take warm Llangollen woollen blankets up to London for re-sale. There the blankets were much appreciated and it soon became apparent both to Edward and his young son, Stephen Lloyd Jones, that there was much profit to be made, more if they were able to manufacture the blankets themselves. And so Mile End Mill was built, taking its name from the Mile End Market in East London where they had sold the Llangollen blankets.

At the point of peak production, Mile End Mill expanded their blanket trade from London to Cardiff, into northern England and Scotland, employing at least forty men. However, disaster struck in the form of an extensive fire which broke out in the weeks before Christmas 1907, gutting the upper storey and destroying most of the roof.

During the rebuilding work, the height of the mill was increased to three storeys, finished with a flat roof and production was resumed. Edward Stephen Jones' daughter, Amy Jane, married a son of the Hughes family of Dee Mills and in 1889, the Lloyd Jones family purchased both Upper and Lower Dee Mills. In c.1920, Upper Dee Mills ceased production and fell slowly into decay. Over the years which followed increasingly limited production continued in the Lower Mill under the direction of William Lloyd Jones, a man of great character and an ardent nationalist of the finest kind.

Many will remember him in old age, making his daily pilgrimage from his home — 'Glanafon' on the Berwyn Road, now the Wild Pheasant Hotel — making slow progress, walking sticks in hand, two elderly sheep dogs following behind, to the almost empty

FESTIVAL OF BRITAIN

Llangollen Chamber of Trade

EXHIBITION
OF

LOCAL INDUSTRIES

AT THE

TOWN HALL
LLANGOLLEN

★

Tuesday, August 21st
TO
Saturday, August 25th
(INCLUSIVE).

★

Opening Ceremony to be performed at
11-30 a.m. on Tuesday, August 21st,
by the President of the Chamber of
Trade, W. CLAYTON RUSSON, Esq.,
M.B.E.

SUPPORTED BY
E. GARNER EVANS, Esq., LI.B., M.P.
H. GLYNNE JONES, Esq.,
Chairman of the Llangollen Chamber of Trade.
J. N. BOWEN, Esq.,
Chairman of the Llangollen Urban District Council

Catalogue, 6d.

Lower Dee Mill.

At the time of the 1951 *Festival of Britain* Llangollen held its own 'Exhibition of Local Industries' in the Town Hall from Tuesday 21st August to Saturday 25th August. This was organised by the Llangollen Chamber of Trade and opened by its President, W. Clayton Russon, Esq., MBE. There were seventeen stands in all, of which only eleven could truly be said to be indigenous.

The introduction to the catalogue made mention of the towns' earlier industries, adding:

"Their decline, besides exerting the more obvious depressing influences, threatened to burden Llangollen with a grievous legacy of eyesores in the shape of deserted buildings in dilapidation and decay — to the detriment of the town's considerable interest in the tourist trade. Instead, happily, the old premises, smartly reconditioned, are humming with new life and adding a welcome diversity to the locality's commerce.
Llangollen, indeed is proving that the proverbially risky procedure of pouring new wine into old bottles can be attended by success."

Stand No. 2 *White Sand & Silica Co., Ltd.*

A perfect example of this is housed in the old slate dressing and processing works at Pentrefelin Wharf. Here, the slate was brought down by tramway from the quarries on top of the Horseshoe Pass. The finished product was taken away by canal and much of the waste was dumped into the river. With the decline of quarrying the premises fell into disuse, the only bright spot coming along with the increase in the popularity of motoring, when a little petrol filling station was erected between the canal and the road, together with the owner's chalet-bungalow.

This, too, is now a thing of the past except for the bungalow, which is now a private residence with forecourt gardens.

It was to the abandoned slate works that the new wine, provided by the White Sand and Silica Company Limited, came in 1940. Their business was to provide ground quartz from sandstone quarried on the Black Mountain near Nerquis and transported to Pentrefelin where modern machinery was installed at a cost of £25,000.

Production began early in 1942 and built up to average 150 tons of ground quartz per week. They supplied the vitreous enamelling market, steel foundries and the fine cement trade, greatly assisting the war effort. Before the Second World War, Britain had depended upon Scandinavia to supply this product.

By the beginning of the 1960s production had almost ceased and the company was employing only one man. Shortly afterwards, the doors were closed and the machinery fell silent. Today, the much-reduced premises house the Llangollen Motor Museum.

Stand No. 3 *The Gwynn Publishing Company*

Founded in 1937 as a new business specialising in the publication of Welsh music by the late W.S. Gwynn Williams, MA and OBE. The company produced the largest catalogue of Welsh music known this century. A great many of its pieces have been used as test pieces at major *Eisteddfodau* and made available to the Llangollen International Musical Eisteddfod (of which Mr. Williams was Musical Director) many of the international classics needed in the choral competitions.

Mr. Williams ran the company from his substantial house, Plas Hafod in Abbey Road, ably assisted by his wife Betty, herself a talented musician and Miss Jenny Madoc Jones.

Stand No. 5 *Caldecot Press Ltd.*
This company manufactured powder proof packets, mostly for Cuthbert's Seeds and Bird's Custard. W. Clayton Russon (who received a knighthood later in his career) set this up in 1941 in the old Tanquery's Brewery in Berwyn Street in conjunction with the 'Seed Factory' (as it was locally known). The name 'Caldecot' came from Caldecot House, Goff's Oak, Herefordshire, which was the original headquarters of Cuthbert's. In 1952 a Midlands-based company took over the Caldecot Press which, after some years, moved to new purpose-built premises across the road, becoming known as Dobson & Crowther Ltd. and now part of the Smurfit Group. At the time of writing, the old brewery premises stand empty.

Stand No. 6 *The Horticultural and Botanical Association Ltd.*
Again founded by the late Sir Clayton Russon in Upper Dee Mill, which he purchased from the Lloyd Jones family in 1941 in semi-derelict condition. As the company prospered, further extensions were built between 1949 and 1960, also purchasing the Abbey Dingle property as trial and experimental grounds. After the death of William Lloyd Jones in 1967, the company purchased Lower Dee Mills from his family.

This became the largest seed factory of its kind in Europe and employed something in the order of 400 people between Llangollen and the smaller Corwen premises. Sadly, all this is now gone with the loss of many jobs within the area. The original Upper Dee Mills is converted to business units, its extensions swept away and the land given over to housing.

Lower Dee Mills houses the 'Doctor Who Experience'. Exactly what William Lloyd Jones would have to say of this, is a matter for speculation — but one can imagine!

Stand No. 7 *Llangollen Tanning Company Ltd.*
Established about the turn of the century in Maesmawr Mills, Church Street and based upon a local industry, which had been in operation for almost one hundred years, the industry was much reliant upon the abundant supply of water provided by the little Cyflymen River. The large, open catchment tanks below Pont Felin Hen were for many years a feature of that end of town.

The main product was Welsh roller skin leather, the use of which was unsurpassed in a great many sections of the cotton industry. During the Second World War the tannery supplied three million feet of leather to be made up into jerkins for the armed forces. Now the 'Lantan' trademark is a thing of the past and once again the site has been developed for private housing. No one however, misses 'the odour', which so often could not be ignored,

especially during the summer months!

Stand No. 9 *Davies Brothers (Motor Supplies) Ltd.*

The Ministry of Supply evacuated this company from Lewisham in south east London at the beginning of 1941. This was owing to the vulnerability of that area to enemy action, which may have put irreplaceable specialised machinery out of production. This would have slowed down the production rate of vital components necessary for the prosecution of the war.

This company was housed in Mile End Mill where it remained after the cessation of hostilities even though the London premises had been returned to production. A quarter of a century later, changing times and internal policy saw a decline in production at Mile End and then its eventual closure. Now the building is divided between canoe products and the restoration of antique beds.

The Broadhurst family, who came up in 1941 to take charge of production at Mile End, first occupied General Yorke's wing of Plas Newydd, leased from the Urban District Council, where they dwelt happily for a good many years. They are still represented within the area.

Stand No. 10 *Dee Valley Frozen Foods Ltd.*

In these days, when the home freezer and frozen foods are an everyday part of housekeeping, it is hard to appreciate that in 1946 the setting up of such a business enterprise in little Llangollen was quite revolutionary. This company, developed as an offshoot of the egg-packing, poultry and farm produce merchants business was established by the Bailey family. They had premises at the junction of Market Street with Berwyn Street (now derelict) and on the corner of Chapel Street with Oak Street (now an antiques shop).

The company specialised in supplying the catering trade with frozen dressed chickens and ducklings, berry fruits, apples and plums, together with green peas and beans. The Chapel Street premises afterwards became showrooms for the Wales Gas Board before being adapted to their present use.

Stand No. 11 *Berwyn Slate Quarries Ltd.*

The slate quarry workings in the Horseshoe Pass area are among the oldest in Wales, having been in production since the Middle Ages. Although major production had ceased by the end of the Second World War, the Berwyn Quarry was a small, newish business involved in the production of specialist products. Some of these were used in the reconstruction of the British Museum and other slab work was supplied for the setting up of the major Festival of Britain Exhibition Centre on London's South Bank.

Today, after a long period of lying fallow, a new company operates again in that windswept place where only the tough survive!

Stand No. 12 *Caefelin Laundry Ltd.*

This once-thriving local business is now the motor repair shop at the top of Market Street. Founded by a local family at the end of the 19th century, the Caefelin Laundry passed into the ownership of the Boote family in 1945 after which time it was much enlarged and modernised to the point of employing in the region of fifty local female staff. Between them they washed 35,000–40,000 articles a week.

Sadly, the business was taken over by a leading national company and thereafter production was slowly diverted away from Llangollen. It is, of course, true that the expectation of almost every household to install their own fully automatic washing machine did much towards sounding the death-knell of the laundry business.

Stand No. 15
This was devoted to the Llangollen Chamber of Trade's Information Bureau and having at that time, as 'a body being only of recent formation' there is little of historic interest to record except perhaps to say that as an organisation, it flourishes still.

Stand No. 16 The *Tuesday Review*
"Llangollen's only strictly local newspaper, and the only one printing completely detailed results of the International Eisteddfod". It was owned, written and published by Miss Sara Pugh Jones, BA, local librarian and historian. Her detailed knowledge of Llangollen and its inhabitants made her the perfect reporter, having the *entrée* to every home.

A Chamber of Trade plaque, c.1952.

Early each Monday morning she would rush to Bala where the paper was printed. She travelled either (at speed) in her red Talbot sports car — known locally as the 'Scarlet Runner' — or, if making the journey by train, on a fiercely-peddled ancient bicycle from her rambling house above the town to Llangollen Station. There would follow a full day of persecuting the printer until all was set up as she required it. Back in Llangollen, her evening would be taken up in sorting the papers into piles, which she would then deliver to all the newsagents of the town before returning home to fold into mail-bands all those copies needed to be sent to Llangollen souls in exile. Finally, a midnight walk down her long drive to the Fron Bache post box, conveniently situated at its gates, saw them safely posted away.

Very sadly, neither the *Tuesday Review* or Sara Pugh Jones are any longer with us. Both a great loss to the town.

For the writer, as a schoolboy

The late Miss Sara Pugh-Jones with the once-famous 'Tuesday Review' (known locally as the 'Llan Punch').

visitor to the 1951 *Festival of Britain* exhibition in the Town Hall, one of the unscheduled delights was being able to examine, at close-quarters, the huge scenic canvas backdrop at the rear of the stage. This depicted an idyllic woodland glade, almost realistic enough to walk into. Some years later, after becoming redundant, it found a new use at Plas Yn Vivod where it was employed in an attempt to counteract drafts at the foot of the staircase in the lower hall/dining room. During the summer months it was, in the manner of a roller blind, drawn up to ceiling level.

Lower Dee Mills, which we now know to have been in decline, did not exhibit. Nor did Llangollen Mill, which we can only imagine had simply chosen not to do so. Another small business, at that time thriving within the town, was the 'Llangollen Pottery', one of the first studio potteries to be established in Wales. From its small beginning upon the premises of the old Waterloo Forge below Waverley Villas, the pottery soon moved into the old slaughterhouse buildings at the rear of 32 Regent Street. Here, in dark corners, rotting sacks of long-forgotten bones still lurked, as did much of the carcass-handling machinery. Perhaps the most acceptable item was a wooden sheep's cradle, which had long stood in the front yard — its end profile was adopted by the pottery as their trademark.

Rhys Powell and his wife Jean first set up the business, but after some few years it floundered financially. To the rescue came the young female partnership of Clare Littleboy and Una Dyer, both art school trained and bursting with much-needed enthusiasm. They gamely took on the business debts, charmed the landlord into allowing them the lease, threw out the old bones and settled down to hard graft. Even their great enthusiasm must have run low at times — especially during the winter months as the building was hardly weatherproof and there were times when the very clay froze. Also, an adequate supply of mains water needed to be piped in and the only affordable way in which this could be done was for the two young ladies to dig the long trench themselves. This they did.

Hard work was finally rewarded and their products became much sought after, winning several Design Centre awards. The premises were made attractive and reasonably comfortable, becoming a favourite place of resort of visitors to the town. Two or three persons were employed, among whom was Eli Breeze who became quite a well-known figure in the 'Prince of Wales' where he would sell home made white clay pipes made across the road, he claimed in his spare time.

Llangollen Pottery in its heyday.

Eventually both partners were seduced by matrimony and the business passed through several hands until purchased by the Lloyd Thomas family who ran it along more commercial lines for some twenty or more years. Now the premises have been converted to attractive courtyard housing and examples of Llangollen Pottery have begun to appear in antique shops at quite competitive prices.

Let it not be assumed that

Una Dyer and Clare Littleboy hard at work in the Llangollen Pottery, 1955.

what has gone before is by any means a complete summary of the commercial life of Llangollen for there were many more businesses, mostly of a smaller nature, to which the strictures of space deny inclusion. Tinsmiths, blacksmiths (the last of these closed his doors in 1952), carpenters and coffin makers — of whom we should mention the family firm of J. Roberts & Sons of Market Street who could, within their carriage works, not only make you a complete vehicle from beginning to end, but also provide a coffin for your departure.

The family of the late Anthony 'Laddie' Jones of Bryn Melyn provided early public transport. Their slogan 'Why Walk?' became famous throughout the town, but curiously as time passed became corrupted by the few into 'Laddie Wire Walks' which was somehow more redolent of the English industrial Midlands.

Robert Hughes & Sons ran a highly successful watch and clockmakers business in Castle Street, which he founded in about 1873 having imported several Coventry craftsmen. At the time of his death in 1895 twenty men were employed, mostly as watchmakers, and although the business was carried on under the direction of his son, R. Ll. Hughes, the manufacture of watches was discontinued in c.1905. Clocks and watches by Robert Hughes & Son may still be discovered, faithfully telling the time within the Llangollen area and further afield.

Coward's Timber Yard was for long a feature in Regent Street. occupying the site now supporting a supermarket.

The late Mr. & Mrs. Llewelyn Hughes. Mrs . Hughes for many years ran the quite fascinating 'Blue Bay' curio and gift shop in Regent Street where many objects of delight were to be found.

Printer's workshops were established in Castle Street (Hugh Jones) and Regent Street (Edwards) but both are now long gone. However, the printing industry, in a new form, is the only major employer of labour in Llangollen today.

Llangollen County School. Main elevation and plan. Architect: Mr. H. Teather.

Education, Schools and Chapels

One of the first mentions of organised education in Llangollen concerns a Dame School kept by a certain Maria Edwards in rooms rented from Mary Williams in her small house beside the long-demolished old Town Hall in Church Street.

Such establishments were often set up by persons who themselves had but scant education and it would seem that Maria divided her attention between teaching and attending to her domestic duties. Both activities took place in the same room where, on Tuesday the 4th March 1739, her husband, dissatisfied by the way in which she had cooked the meat, murdered her in front of her pupils. Let us hope that she was a better teacher than cook!

In 1827 the invaluable W.T. Simpson informs us that "in the Churchyard is a school, under which is a vestry room bearing the inscription This Schoolhouse was built at the expense of the Parishioners having obtained the ordinary licence; with consent of the Rev: R. Price, Vicar, 1773". Therefore, it would seem that the educational needs of at least some of the town's young were taken care of from quite early times. The school was endowed by the three bequests, details of which can be read in the north aisle of the Church.

In 1840 this had developed into the Old National School to be seen on the right upon entering the Hand Hotel drive from Regent Street where a plaque declares 'For the promotion of the education of the poor in the principles of the established Church'. A British School was established, first in the old Rehoboth Chapel before moving into its own new building in Brook Street — now the Penllyn Mission Chapel.

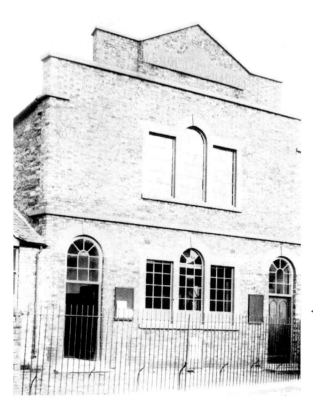

The former British School, Brook. Now the Penllyn Chapel.

Attendance, it would seem, was generally very poor at both establishments for in January 1846 an inspection was made finding that at the National School only fifty-eight out of a registered ninety-eight pupils were present. At the British School a mere one hundred and forty-seven were in attendance out of a possible two hundred and twenty-two. It would seem that had one hundred percent attendance ever been achieved, both buildings would have suffered from over crowding! The Headmaster's logbook has an entry for 21st March 1866:

"The room being so full, found it impossible to put the children to sit far enough from each other when writing from dictation: A new classroom is a great desideratum."

The logbook also gives sundry reasons for poor attendance:

"May 13th 1864. Alexander Reid Esquire gave permission for the poor to carry firewood from Fedwddu for eight days — as many of my scholars were sent by their parents for the wood — this partly accounts for my average being less than usual this week.

September 12th 1864. A circus affected the attendance — I had only twelve in school in the afternoon therefore I did not mark them in the Register.

April 21st 1865. The attendance much affected owing to the opening of the Llangollen & Corwen Railway.

June 5th 1865. Very few in School this morning. No school in the afternoon owing to the annual feast of the Eagles Friendly Society."

However, there was a legitimate reason for absence on 5th April 1872:
"All the schools of the town treated with tea on the occasion of the marriage of Miss Wagstaffe of Plas Yn Vivod. Expenses defrayed by Mr. Wagstaffe."

The children of these schools were also treated to Mander's Menagerie, which was exhibiting in the town on that day.

Following the Education Act of 1870 the National School was greatly enlarged and the new building opened in October 1873, with a procession led by a drum and fife band. Afterwards followed a tea party and a Welsh sermon, which no doubt delighted the young pupils! The following year, again in October, the newly-built Board School in

Llangollen Board School, Girls' Group III. Year unknown.

Parade Street was opened, this time with a procession led by the Llansantffraid Brass Band, no doubt followed by tea, but as far as one knows without the benefit of a Welsh sermon.

Today, the National School is part Llangollen Health Centre and part Church Hall. The Board School now being largely occupied by the European Centre for Traditional & Regional Cultures (ECTARC) but does, however, retain some link with its former use in as much as the 'Victorian School Museum' is housed in one wing. Both former schools are incorporated in the new Ysgol Bryn Collen at Pengwern.

There were, of course, a number of private schools about the town including those at Thornleigh, Green Lodge and The Tower, but the most notable of these was Walton House School, precursor of Llangollen Intermediate or County School.

In 1887 J. Lias Davies of Nantyr, whose great ambition had been to obtain a place at Oxford University, found to his great disappointment that this was not possible, regardless of his having studied Classics at Aberystwyth University College for four years. Unfortunately, he had not taken a degree there, feeling that to become an Oxford graduate would greatly enhance his standing. Undaunted, he decided to open a school in Llangollen and was fortunate in being able to rent Walton House from Mr. John Rowlands, a successful grocer with a great enthusiasm for education. The school was opened in late September 1887 and was unique in its day, as the following reminiscence written by the late John Rees Thomas, MA explains:

"The pupils of Walton School from 1889 to 1893 were a very strange mixture; ages ranged from eleven to twenty years; we were sons of farmers, tradesmen, hotel proprietors, factory and quarry owners, gentlemen of independent means, together

with six or seven adult ministerial students preparing for the entrance examinations of the various denomentural colleges. Altogether we were about thirty in number. As we were all of different attainments, ages, entering the school at different times, class teaching was practically impossible. Each pupil worked by himself and pursued his studies under the direction of Mr. Lias Davies. In spite of all the variety and divergence, we were all animated with the same enthusiasm and keenness for work. Mr. Lias Davies possessed in a remarkable degree the gift of being able to stimulate his pupils to personal and individual effort. He knew how to create the necessary atmosphere. His bright and winsome personality irritated all. He ruled with a gentle yet firm hand.

Parents who could not for various reasons send their children to Ruabon Grammar School, Grove Park, Wrexham, or the High School, Oswestry [Mr. Owen Owen's old school] *were glad to avail themselves of the facilities offered them by Mr. Lias Davies and all were delighted with the benefit their children received at Walton School.*

(signed) John Rees Thomas, MA, Nottingham.

Later, the Reverend Robert Davies, brother of J. Lias, joined the school, taking charge of the juniors. Miss Renshaw of Sheffield married Lias Davies in 1891 and set up a school for girls, thus making Walton House, in today's terms, a co-educational secondary school. Pupils were prepared for the examinations of the College of Preceptors, London Matriculation and for entrance scholarships to college and university. It is a matter of great credit to Walton House School that the above-mentioned John Rees Thomas was a star pupil, being second in all England in the College of Preceptors examination for his particular year, going on to obtain his MA at London University.

In 1889 the Welsh Intermediate Education Act was passed and a committee was immediately formed to:

"Take steps to endeavour to secure the Establishment of an Intermediate School for the district of Llangollen, Chirk, Glyn Traian, Llansantffraid, Glyn Ceiriog and Llantysilio."

A number of meetings were held from time to time and subscription lists were opened to obtain donations towards the school building fund. The Denbighshire Education Scheme received Queen Victoria's approval in August 1894 and it promised to pay the sum of £1,600 out of the County Building Fund for the erection of suitable school buildings, provided that the Llangollen catchment area could raise £800 by voluntary donations.

By New Year's Day 1895 the sum of eight hundred and five pounds, eighteen shillings and ninepence had been raised by public subscription and a board of governors of sixteen 'worthies' set up. Mr. E. Ffoulkes-Jones was appointed Clerk to the Governors, the joint Treasurers being Mr. John Morris of Maesmawr House and Mr. Edward Roberts, Fronhyfryd.

In January 1895, the Governors issued a statement of progress, which expressed the opinion that £2,400 was:

"... to small a sum to provide buildings of such a character as will worthily represent the movement. The Governors are of the opinion that at least £3,000 should be raised. Therefore, they appeal to the public for the further amount required and, encouraged by enthusiasm and unanimity which has been displayed in this matter throughout, confidently look forward to a generous response so as to

assure to Llangollen and district the boon of a County School, the want of which has been long and keenly felt."

The Governors went on to add that they were taking steps to open the school in temporary buildings which they did in Plas Geraint, a large property between Hall Street and Berwyn Street, later to become the Post Office. This building had previously housed the Baptist Theological College until it was transferred to Bangor to be closer to the University. The opening of the school took place on Wednesday 8th May 1895, there then being no further need for Walton House, which was advertised to be let in *Llangollen Advertiser* January 15th 1897. Mr. Lias Davies, whose teaching gifts were remarkable, was appointed Classics Master at the new school of which he had donated two guineas towards the cost of building. It should be pointed out that the 'Plas Geraint' referred to here is not to be confused with the large white monumental house at the foot of the Geraint, to which the name was later transferred.

Meanwhile, the task of raising extra monies for the building of the new school continued with some success. The site known as Pen y Bont Field was purchased and the first sod cut by Mrs. Myddleton Biddulph of Chirk Castle on the 22nd June 1897. James Darlington Esq., of Black Park laid the foundation stone on 21st September of the same year. The building was constructed of best Ruabon red brick as manufactured by the J.C. Edwards Brickworks. Mr. Edwards had been one of the first to respond to the original building fund appeal with a handsome donation of £20.

Construction was completed in 1898 at a cost of £4,090, with an extra £700 being spent on the building of the Headmaster's house. On September 21st 1898 the new County School was officially opened by the Honourable G.T. Kenyon, thus providing Llangollen with the finest of intermediate schools, "the want of which has been long and keenly felt".

The first Headmaster was Henry R. Olley, BA Camb. Inter Arts, London 21st Wrangler, late Mathematical Scholar of St Peters College, Cambridge, Gilchrist and Goldsmith Scholar, Prizeman and Exhibitioner of London University. It would appear he was quite well qualified!

He graciously presided over this fine new building which promised "first class modern education for boys and girls. Thoroughness of work secured. Chemical Laboratory, Cookery and Laundry work and work shop, playfield, and preparation for examination. Tuition Fee, £5 per Annum".

Children from the outlying areas such as Glyn Ceiriog, would be placed with local families as midweek boarders, going home for weekends and school holidays. At the time of opening the school had only seventy registered pupils, which was something of a disappointment as provision had been made for one hundred and twenty, but numbers soon began to increase.

Unlike headteachers of today Mr. Olley could not have lived any closer to his school, an arrangement he obviously found to be of great convenience.

The late Emrys Haddon Roberts, a distinguished pupil and old boy who went on to become Head of Grove Park School, Wrexham returned to distribute prizes and certificates for the Speech Day ceremony in 1964. During the course of his speech he paid affectionate tribute to his old Headmaster:

"He was known to appear in carpet slippers for the first Mathematics lesson of the morning, but taught Italian method and Standard Form as no other. He even occasionally slipped back to the School House to finish his breakfast and really did give us a half holiday which had the delightful quality of dropping out of the blue

Llangollen County School Old Pupils' Association at their annual gathering, June 14th 1906. Mr. Olley is front row, centre.

Llangollen County School in about 1907. Mr. Olley appears left of centre below the large gentleman with receding hair

when someone got a Bangor Scholarship, not like today's speaker at speech day who asks merely as a matter of form for one which has to be filched from twelve weeks and ten days.
On his grave at Llantysilio Churchyard, they put a piece of rough-hewn granite with the single word 'Resurgam'. Henry R. Olley was a great Headmaster."

Under his guidance the County School prospered and in 1913 a new science building was opened to which children from other schools in the town and outlying districts were allowed to come up for lessons in domestic science and woodwork. Two World Wars came and went before any further building took place, but a new kitchen and dining hall were finally provided, being opened by Mrs. M.A. Hughes (Westhoe) on 8th May 1945.

The exclusive spirit of a County School was lost under the 1944 Education Act whereby all pupils in the area over the age of eleven were given every opportunity to develop their aptitudes. Llangollen became a Grammar School in 1945 followed by a major change to bilateral school in 1960. New buildings were built and a new name given — Ysgol Dinas Brân. And what changes since! The original building has been swept away to make room for a confusion of modern buildings which no longer present any pretence of living in harmony together. No place now for dear Mr. Olley in his carpet slippers!

Wales has, as a nation, a long-held tradition of self-improvement by dint of diligent self-education. In this the libraries have played no small part, Llangollen being particularly fortunate in as much as it was one of the first towns to have a Public Library. Even before this, there had been a good library housed at the Workingman's Institute, above the old Post Office in Bridge Street since at least 1848.

The Public Library occupied two large ground floor rooms within the Town Hall building (now the Town Clerk's offices) and was officially opened in October 1886. Largely supported by public subscriptions, concerts, and Shakespeare reading by the famous actress Helen Faucit, wife of Sir Theodore Martin, himself a generous subscriber and donator of books. Many other books were donated by Mr. Lockett of Pen y Bryn and several other local people, including some fine first editions.

At the annual meeting of the Llangollen Public Library and Newsroom held on 8th January 1897. The treasurer, Mr. G. Williams, announced that having begun the year with an adverse balance of seven pounds, five shillings and one penny, the library was at last in credit to the tune of twelve shillings! Redemption it seems had come by way of the proceeds of a lecture and concert arranged by Mr. Ralph Darlington, and a generous donation of £5 from Lady Martin. The librarian, Miss Bessie Jones, felt that the corner had been turned and that this, together with the recent substantial additions to the book stock, boded well for the future.

And so it continued under the care of such subsequent librarians as Mr. W.H. Jones and the redoubtable but kindly Miss Sara Pugh Jones until the Urban District Council decided that the interests of the library would be best served by joining forces with the County Library Services. In a letter dated 3rd December 1959 the Town Clerk wrote, very officially, to the librarian:

"In view of the relinquishment of the Council's Library powers to the Denbighshire County Council on the 1st April 1960, I am directed to instruct you to cease purchasing any further books for the Public Library.
I am also directed to terminate the contract with Foyles Libraries Ltd. as at 2nd January 1960 and I am writing to them today."

Thereafter, things changed quickly. Llangollen Library had been a comfortable,

homely place with something of the atmosphere of a gentleman's club — long established, if perhaps a little old-fashioned. Classical busts and brass candelabra graced the
tops of the book stacks. Large, oak-framed dignitaries and sepia scenes of an earlier
Llangollen hung from the walls and children were charmed by the enormous gilt-framed
oil painting of a Boxer dog and kittens, which occupied the wall space above the librarian's desk. A commodious, antique octagonal table littered with magazines and a comfortable chair for a waiting mum stood between desk and door. In its centre a vase of
fresh-cut flowers from Bryndedwydd garden. Altogether, the very effect which interior
designers of today strive so hard to achieve.

However, the designers of the sixties were of a very different mind. The mood of the
day was 'out with anything old — make way for minimalist new'. This look was known
as 'contemporary' — what else could it have been? The County Librarian was, it seems,
in tune with the times and so the metamorphosis began. Out went all the 'clutter'.
Familiar framed faces were soon to look at only the dusty interiors of dark storerooms.
Old glass-fronted bookcases disappeared and were replaced with plain, new, open ones.
Everything was painted in either a curious shade of salmon pink, or queasy yellow-
green.

Many townsfolk muttered — but not too loudly, perhaps thinking it not too high a
price to pay for a plentiful supply of new 'westerns' or good 'romances' with which to
relax after washing day. But when it became apparent that the removal of the collection
of fine old books was imminent, many voices were raised in anger. It must be remembered that many of these were finely bound 18th and 19th century volumes, often first
editions, donated from the libraries of people such as Sir Theodore and Lady Martin and
their friend the poet Robert Browning who had together donated nearly 1,000 volumes.
Many letters were written and representations made through the local librarian who was
herself distressed by the turn of events.

The County Librarian, in a difficult position which he was forced to defend, eventually found himself being interviewed by BBC Radio Wales. Perhaps caught a little off his
guard, he made the statement in defence of uniform new volumes in plastic covers that
"no one wants to read dirty books"! The wags of the town afterwards being heard to
declare that they had spent years looking for dirty books in Llangollen Library!

A compromise was, however, eventually reached. The branch was allowed to keep one
case of old books on condition that these could be said to be of local importance. Some
were given to the National Library of Wales, who could only accept those which they did
not already have, and the remainder were unceremoniously dumped in Cell 13 at Ruthin
Jail, the then headquarters of the County Library Service. Here they were to languish
before being fed to the boilers. Further pressure from the local librarian brought the con-
cession that she could remove as many books as she could manage in the space of one
hour, on condition that none were to find there way back into Llangollen Library.

And so, quite early one Saturday morning, Miss Pugh-Jones and a friend sped over
the Horseshoe Pass on a rescue mission, returning with the back of the famous 'Scarlet
Runner' piled high with reference volumes. Much time having been lost from the pre-
cious hour in the seeking out of all volumes belonging to three or six book sets.

Miss Sara Pugh Jones continued as librarian in charge of Llangollen branch until her
retirement in 1967 when Mr. L.G. Sherratt, who had been Deputy Librarian for several
years, succeeded her. At this time, Llangollen had become a full-time branch, i.e. open
for five-and-a-half days per week. The people of Llangollen organised a surprise party
to honour Miss Pugh-Jones, at which she was presented with a typewriter, a framed
antique watercolour of her beloved Llangollen and a quite substantial cheque.

Llangollen Library soon after the County take-over. Miss S. Pugh-Jones behind the desk.

In 1971 the County, having purchased and demolished the Conservative Club in Parade Street, used the site to erect a new purpose-built Library of singular design. It must be said that the old premises were not exactly convenient, at least from the point of view of the librarian and staff, there being no separate office and all business having to be conducted from behind the corner reception desk. Behind this was the only convenience — a small Victorian hand basin (cold water only) beneath which the librarian had provided his own small metholated spirit stove and kettle for the much-needed occasional cup of tea. The lavatory was communal and reached by ascending upwards of thirty stone steps, making it quicker and more convenient to rush into the Police Station next door.

The new Library was officially opened on Thursday 16th November 1971, the librarian having resigned the previous September, unable to cope with the comforts offered by the new building after the Spartan conditions enjoyed across the road. His successor was Miss Ann Owen from Montgomeryshire, who had studied the Bibliographical Organisation of Welsh Language and Literature at Aberystwyth. Thus began a new chapter in the story of Llangollen Library.

Moral education was taken care of by the various and numerous places of worship within the town. The place of the Church has been fully dealt with and was augmented about 1870 when Eglwys y Ddol, built in 1858 as a cemetery Chapel, took on a full-time roll as Saint John's Welsh Church, to which all Welsh services previously held in the parish Church were transferred. However, a very important part was played by the Nonconformist movement without the help and guidance of whom many prominent

Welshmen may never have had the opportunity to develop their talents.

It is known that the famous John Wesley passed through Llangollen in 1789. He did not preach, but two years later Evan Roberts of Denbigh most certainly did. Bravely, he took up a stand in the main street and began to sing in a rich, melodious voice which so intrigued the people that a crowd gathered about him in very little time. Seizing the moment, Evan Roberts began his sermon, which quickly gathered momentum until being rudely interrupted by a male onlooker determined to disrupt the proceedings. Another, having a laudable sense of fair play, seized the troublemaker and unceremoni- ously sent him on his way, to the great pleasure of the crowd. The sermon was heard to its conclusion without any further interruption and had so delighted the congregation that they made a collection among themselves, which they offered to the preacher. Evan Roberts expressed his gratitude but said that he would prefer the money to be given to the poor of the town.

In August 1801 the Wesleyan preacher Mr. Bryan visited Llangollen and preached with such fervour that there were many conversions. Among them was John Jones of Llangollen Mill, a noted cock-fighter who upon returning home greatly surprised his wife by going out to the yard and decapitating all his birds, said to be the finest in the county, in order to rid himself of temptation. By 1802 the Welsh Methodist Society was formed, the first members being John Jones the miller and his wife; Mr. & Mrs. J. Bowen, Dinbren; Mr. & Mrs. J. Edwards, Shoemaker; Mary Evans, Plas Ifan and her two daugh- ters; J. Williams, Wern Uchaf; Mr. & Mrs. Edward Williams; and Edward Jones of Llantysilio.

Capel Pentre Morgan was built in Hall Street in 1804. The building still stands, form- ing part of the row of cottages opening directly onto the pavement opposite to the rear of the Post Office. This small but intimate place of worship served until a new Chapel was built at the corner of Castle Street and Berwyn Street, imposingly set in a garden protected by iron railings. This was in turn replaced by the present Capel 'Seion', a much larger building, which was opened on 13th August 1905 and is still in use today.

At the other end of town is the little Chapel known affectionately as 'The Shack'. The famous Thomas Charles of Bala had preached during one of his tours through North Wales in the 1780s. Ironically, this curious little building became a brewery in the 19th century, which must have caused sore distress within the cause.

Another early small Chapel was Glan yr Afon, situated close to the river and approached by the narrow driveway between Stafford House and the old Talbot Inn. The newer Glanrafon Welsh Independent Chapel situated on the Victorian promenade closed its doors in the late 1970s and was offered for sale. Because of its prime location facing the river it seemed likely that the future would be at the very least uncertain, but a small Christian group mercifully, and rather heroically, came to the rescue and the Chapel con- tinues their work today.

Victoria Square is graced by the impressive façade of Chapel Rehoboth, the former home of Welsh Calvinistic Methodism. The present Chapel is an enlargement of the orig- inal, the work having been completed in 1874 at a cost of £1,153. Thinking to build a completely new Chapel, the trustees had first bought a large plot of land beside the Police Station from Mr. Henry Robertson but decided to release this for the building of the Board School. Today, Rehoboth is owned by a company engaged in the restoration of antique beds. It is much to their credit that the fine façade remains intact and is no way disfigured by hoardings.

The English Baptist movement was first represented by the building of Pen y Bryn Chapel above Hill Street. It is now demolished, but the little burial ground remains. The

A mystery photograph! The author has two copies — one bears the inscription "Glan Yr Afon Chapel group in 1884", none of which is correct. The other is captioned "Llangollen Choral Society..." (which it IS) "...at Llantysilio Hall" (which it clearly is NOT!).

Doctor Pritchard Memorial Chapel on Abbey Road was built to replace this and now forms part of the Bryn Melyn garage complex. Doctor Pritchard was highly respected within the town and had been secretary of the British School from the time of its foundation until its transference to the Board. He died, aged 80, on 7th September 1875.

As we know, the British School became the Penllyn Mission Chapel and continues to be so at the time of writing. Capel y Beddwrn, the Welsh Baptist Chapel, commands a prominent position in Castle Street and was built in 1860 when this area of the town was first being developed. The fine façade remains more or less intact, although a new brick forecourt replaces the original little garden then approached through fine wrought-iron gates. At the time of its conversion from Chapel into exhibition and performance area for ECTARC, it was proposed to disfigure the frontage by the addition of a bow-fronted glass metal excrescence at first floor level. This plan provoked much opposition within the town and was mercifully abandoned.

Captain William Paul, a devout Methodist and man of Cornwall came to Llangollen in the mid-19th century to establish the Pentre Slateworks at Pentrefelin and could well be regarded as the founder of English-speaking Methodism in this area. For such information as we have concerning this, we are largely indebted to the Reverend J. Roger Roberts.

It would seem that Captain Paul and a few friends first worshipped in the former's home but resolved to build a Chapel "suitable for the accommodation of visitors and resident friends". The result was the building now known as the Memorial Hall in Market Street and was first erected as a Chapel capable of seating one hundred and fifty persons. The foundation stone was laid in September 1862 and the Chapel, built at a cost of four hundred and eleven pounds, five shillings and sixpence was opened on the 21st August 1863. The Chapel proved to be exceedingly popular and, regardless of being extended in 1890, was found to be too small to accommodate the extra influx of visitors during the summer months.

*Building work in progress on the English Methodist
Church in 1903.*

THE NEW

Welsh Wesleyan Methodist Church,
LLANGOLLEN.

BAZAAR,

SEPTEMBER, 1912.

CHAIRMAN:
Rev. W. RICHARD ROBERTS, Superintendent Minister.
VICE-CHAIRMAN:
E. R. PARRY, Esq., J.P., C.C.
TREASURERS:
Mr. EDWARD DAVIES, Cambrian Terrace.
Mr. JOHN WILLIAMS, Bryngwyn.
SECRETARIES:
Mr. P. LLOYD HUMPHREYS, Spring Bank.
Mr. J. WATKIN ROBERTS, Penlan.

HUGH JONES, PRINTER, LLANGOLLEN.

At a trustees meeting on the 20th December 1901
Mr. Ralph Darlington proposed the building of a new
Church and the Reverend J. Seawall Haworth generously made a gift of the present site between the
Riverside Walk and Princess Street. Here the fine
new Church, so often portrayed on calendars and
picture postcards, was erected at a cost of £4,264
and was opened on the 24th March 1904. It remains
a popular place of worship to this day.

Over the years, there has been a sad decline in
Church and Chapel attendance with the result that
many of these fine buildings have, of necessity,
ceased to fulfil the purpose for which they were
built. The best hope is that new owners will
respect what they stand for and do all in their
power to at least preserve the exteriors of these
buildings which previous generations, through
personal sacrifice and determined dedication,
fought so hard to build.

An open air tea party held on the field behind Dolafon Villas. Event unknown.

Leisure, Pleasure & Social Amenities

"**S**imple pleasures are the best", the 'I want-ing' child was always told, and simple pleasures were always the only ones available to the townsfolk of early Llangollen. Most organised activities took place upon the Green and were, of course, very much dependent upon the weather. Games and dancing constituted the main activities and later it became fashionable to hold archery competitions. Butts and straw targets were set up, with the spectators safely positioned out of arrow's reach — competition could become intense. Some were known to shoot wide, especially those from the hands of the inexperienced, and also depending on the amount of good Llangollen ale that had been consumed!

Each year there was a large and popular fair held in the month of March and this was much looked forward to. These fairs took the form of street markets with the addition of entertainers — jugglers, acrobats, etc. and, of course, pickpockets!

The Winter Fair was much affected by the weather but was nevertheless an event not to be missed. Lady Eleanor Butler recorded in her diary on Tuesday 22nd November 1782:

"White glittering frost. Country magnificently beautiful. A Fair in the village. What a picture might be drawn from our Parlour window of the crowds descending the opposite mountain and passing through the field before our cottage. Some on horseback, many on foot, all comfortably clad, each bringing their different commodity to the Fair, as cattle, pigs, poultry, eggs, cheese, baskets, woodenware, spinning wheels. The women knitting as they went along, the young people in their best apparel; health, content and innocence illuminating every countenance, all

Market Day *by Griffiths.*

speeding with heartfelt joy to Llangollen. Mary in her glory, purchasing beef for hanging, and exerting all her powers of eloquence in bargaining with the butchers."

Having walked all the way over the mountain from the Ceiriog Valley, Mary and her family were no doubt looking forward to hot chestnuts and baked potatoes to warm their hands and innards!

In 1800 Lady Eleanor was not enamoured of the March Fair, describing it as the poorest she had known since she had come to Wales:

"Neither Beef nor Veal, the price of meat being so exorbitant that few can afford to purchase it. Many market days formerly were better attended, greater number of buyers and sellers than there are this Fair."

Edward I granted Llangollen a charter issued from Caernarfon on 16th July 1284. It allowed the holding of two fairs a year and a weekly market within the town. For many years the existence of this document seems to have been forgotten and in the late 1960s the Urban District Council decided, in their wisdom, to ban the holding of the regular Tuesday market to free the area for extra parking. Somehow, the ancient Charter — which can only be repealed by Act of Parliament — made a miraculous reappearance and the market continues to be held.

In common with many other towns it was also the custom to hold an annual Wake during the month of June to celebrate the feast of Saint Collen. Lady Eleanor records this with a rather barbed entry in her journal for 7th June 1790:

"We walked before the door to behold the multitude of happy and well drest people in groups from all the neighbouring towns and villages, assembling to the Wakes of Llangollen. These Wakes, not withstanding the badness of the weather, are the best

we remember these many years. The men are very well drest, all in new apparel. The women the same but less ridiculous, more consistent with the simplicity of their situation!"

Later the same year they sent a man to the village to bring up a traveller with a performing bear to be exhibited in their front field. The animal was said to be huge, but tame and of the female sex, being named Nancy. No doubt it was also considered to be properly dressed, for it pleased the Ladies who fed it with bread and mutton and small beer! One hopes that the master was equally rewarded.

Travelling freak shows and acting troops were also popular entertainment, regardless of the quality of the performance. By the mid-19th century, Ginetts Circus was a regular visitor to Llangollen and the Fairs had become more sophisticated — but not all was to the liking of John Griffiths, Headmaster of the British School, who recorded the following observation on 20th March 1865:

"The electrogalvanic batteries, photographic studios, whirligigs and swings were innocent enough but most of the shows, tumbling, boxing, gambling etc were to be condemned. Many of the stereoscopic views were decidedly indecent. In one part we observed a man! deceiving the public by pretending to put silver in a purse and selling it and its contents for one shilling. There is a vulgarity, a want of mental elevation in such practices which might induce an intelligent man to reprobate them even if the voices of morality and religion were silent."

Perhaps he did not enjoy his visit.

In April 1897 'A ratepayer' complained in a letter to the *Llangollen Advertiser* of travelling showmen who did not keep decent hours and that the letting of the Smithfield to such people was becoming a source of great nuisance:

"I do not complain about the organgrinding, although that when at it continually all day, approaches very near to the unbearable. But I do object to the gun reports and to the noise inseparable with the pulling down of such concerns when carried on late at night and in the early hours of the morning. There was brisk shooting going on between twelve and one o'clock on Tuesday morning, while the following night the hammering and other noises incidental to pulling down kept me awake for hours."

One man's pleasure — another's pain! As a result, the Council decided that the Smithfield should only be let for such purposes on the condition that "the noises be discontinued from 7–8 p.m. and then at 10 p.m. on week nights, except on Saturday night at 11 p.m.".

Hunting, shooting and fishing have long been held as popular pursuits for the countryman. If unable to afford to hunt there is much pleasure to be had from hunt following and, similarly, it costs nothing to beat — indeed, one would normally be paid to do so. Fishing is open to all and has always been popular in Llangollen, especially when the Dee was famous as a salmon river.

For Arthur G. Bradley, who wrote in praise of the Vale in 1898, there was no greater pleasure than a visit to John Roberts, "the sanctum of the veteran salmon-slayer, coraclist, rod-maker, fly-tier". His cottage was distinguished by the sign of a "gilt perch hanging from an impossible rod — no conventional tackle shop, with a plate-glass window and a counter, but an old Welsh cottage parlour with low oak ribbed ceilings, and walls two feet thick, and a huge chimney and a deep-set window".

A coracle fisherman, Mr. Deryn Jones, receiving his sustaining 'pintas' from Mr. O.A. Walker, the Dairy, in c.1956.

For many of us, the description would almost fit the premises of the late 'Miss Lewis Fishing Tackle' at the top of Chapel Street, now a restaurant. Others may remember her earlier title 'Miss Lewis Paris Fashion's', stemming from younger days, when she and her sister modelled smart 'modern' gowns and accessories at the Hand Hotel (c.1920). The little shop ably supplied all the visiting and local fisherman's needs, save perhaps a coracle.

Coracle fishermen had since early times been a familiar sight on the Llangollen Dee, sadly disappearing not too many years ago. The craft was quite crudely constructed from ash or hazel to form the framework over which was stretched waterproofed tarpaulin. Flat-bottomed, and with a basic plank seat, the craft was light and so could be carried to and from the river by means of a leather strap about the shoulders. This gave the fisherman the appearance of a giant turtle. In recent years the Dee, in common with many other rivers, has suffered from depleted salmon stocks.

The Vale of Llangollen Harriers flourished in the 1890s and beyond. They centred on the Eglwyseg and Vivod areas, meeting at the Old Kennels, The Drum (Eglwyseg Rocks) and the Keeper's Cottage. Otter hounds were kept in kennels near Dinbren Hall (below Y Wylfa) on the bank of the small River Brân.

Someone once calculated that Llangollen had more societies and committees than any town of comparable size within the British Isles! This would seem to have held good since at least the mid-19th century and the tradition has survived up to the present day. Every Church and Chapel — and there were many — had their own societies, guilds and bands, all of which were well supported.

Amateur Operatic, Choral and Dramatic Societies provided entertainment, and the popular Llangollen Amateur Minstrel Troupe gave benefit concerts in the Town Hall Assembly Rooms. Magic lantern lectures were very popular and, being often of an 'improving nature', the venue was very often a Chapel or Schoolroom. These were also provided as entertainment at children's tea parties, making a welcome change from the almost compulsory pupil participation concerts at which the 'talents' of the young were displayed. Such public exhibitions may well have delighted the parents, but were often purgatory to the pupils who dared not refuse to perform. Perhaps they had heard of the fate of the young boy from Froncysyllte School who had been expelled in February 1898 for refusing to "state the reason why he did not sing when requested to do so by his teacher".

At a tea for the town's schoolchildren given at the Town Hall Assembly Rooms on 21st March 1874 the entertainment was of a singularly intriguing nature. A series of

Welsh Literary Society players.

'Dissolving Views' especially adapted for children were exhibited by W.H. Darby Esq. and J.C.E. Darby Esq. Sadly, we shall never know the details of this as all those present are now themselves dissolved. It is interesting to note that the Brothers Darby were descendants of the great Ironmaster, Abraham Darby, of Coalbrookdale. They had joined forces with Henry Robertson to found the Brymbo Iron Company in 1846.

Outdoor pursuits were not forgotten. Llangollen has long-established (and notable) football and cricket clubs. Later on, tennis became a popular pastime and courts were provided in the Riverside Park and beside the Canal. Bowling greens were laid at Plas Newydd and the riverside as well as in the Ponsonby Gardens. Swimmers had to be con-tent with the cold, rushing river. The very brave could — and still can — be observed making breath-taking dives from the Town Bridge. Not to be recommended.

The Victoria Promenade was opened in 1899 to com-memorate the Diamond Jubilee of Queen Victoria after rather protracted negotiations with Mr. Dicken of Tyn Dwr Hall (the owner of the land) and with Mr. M.H. Roberts (regarding his

Llangollen Cricket Club in 1928.

Riverside Walk, c.1900.

adjacent property). This became a very popular area locally. The less energetic simply occupying one of the many seats facing the river and enjoying a cheerful word with the promenaders. Summer Sunday evenings saw groups of the local young, dressed in their best, surveying the scene — and each other. Many a good match was made there.

Later, this popular walk was extended into the Riverside Park complete with bandstand, paddling pool and children's play area. There were tennis courts for the energetic and good greens for the more leisurely game of bowls.

Llangollen's Silver Band was well known within the area, winning many prizes and was a great summer attraction for both visitors and locals alike. They made good use of the new bandstand where they played to large audiences on sunny summer afternoons. Walkers on the new Cerrig y Llan footpath, which extended as far as Mile End before being eroded by floods in later years, could enjoy their music from a distance. The band has survived well over the years and may often be heard practising stentoriously within their hut on Parade Street.

Indoors, the Pavilion Theatre catered for concerts, plays and similar on a rather more business-like basis than the facilities existing in the Town Hall Assembly Room. Built about 1900, this large palace of delights, largely of corrugated iron construction, occupying the site between Hall Street and Berwyn Street, is now a petrol filling station. It was able to accommodate large capacity audiences, equalled by extensive platform facilities. For example, a performance of 'Judas – Maccabeus' given there on Tuesday 11th February 1902, boasted a "Band & Chorus of 120 performers". The best seats were two shillings and sixpence each. After the performance a special train left Llangollen Station for Ruabon and intermediate stations at 10.15 p.m. The Llangollen Choral Society, under the baton of Mr. R. Wilfred Jones, ARAM gave the performance. A glance at the programme revealed that the 'Band' was really an orchestra augmented by Mr. C.H. Williams on harmonium and Miss Lloyd Jones at the piano.

Llangollen Silver Band, c.1895.

In later years the Pavilion fell into decline but did enjoy a revival with the advent of cinema. It is said that in its final years a combination of slovenly cleaning and the newly fashionable potato crisp encouraged rats to scamper between the feet of the audience after the house lights had been dimmed.

After this the needs of cinema goers were catered for by Mr. Horspool's much grander 'Dorothy Cinema' and the Pavilion became the Jones Brothers garage.

There were very few motor cars to be seen about Llangollen in the early days. Mr. Harry Best of Plas yn Vivod recalled his father having bought his first car, an Argyle CA 23, in April 1908. But his grandfather had amazed the neighbourhood by the purchase of a steam car in September 1898. This was manufactured by the Lancashire Steam Motor Company of Leyland, being guaranteed to climb a gradient of 1 in 7 and could carry sufficient water for a five-hour run. Apparently, it did climb the Horseshoe Pass — with several stops and a fill of water at Oernant. However, the oil burners proved to be most unsatisfactory and it would frequently jump out of gear, so it was returned to the manufacturers.

Another Argyle motor car came to Llangollen at about the same time as Captain

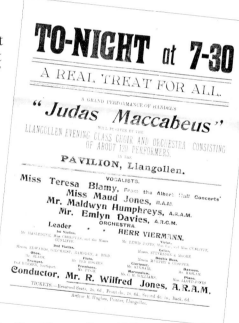

Pavilion Theatre flyer, 1902.

Best's, having being purchased from the company's motor works at Bridgetown near Glasgow by Mr. Robertson of Plas Newydd. A Mr. Knox, an employee of the company, delivered the motor car to Llangollen. He afterwards allowed himself to be persuaded by the Robertson's to stay on as their chauffeur/mechanic. Mr. Knox took convenient lodgings with Mr. & Mrs. Jones of Min Nant at the bottom of Butler Hill. He recalled an occasion upon which, having collected the two Miss Robertson's from the station, found upon reaching the foot of Hill Street the way to be blocked by a slow-moving funeral procession and so decided to attempt the steep ascent of Butler's Hill. Many people stood open-mouthed to see if he would reach the top — mercifully, he did.

At that time it was a finable offence to drive a motor car at a speed in excess of ten miles per hour. However, Knox liked a turn of speed and would go out at night along the main road as far as the Gobowen boundary in order to test the Argyle's maximum speed, of twenty-five miles per hour, between the mile stones. The vehicle was also used to pull a large mower for the cutting of Plas Newydd lawns — a task previously allotted to a pony, who would wear special leather shoes.

Plas Newydd lawns were also the usual venue for the crowning of the May Queen or Maid of the Vale. This much looked-forward to carnival procession was for many years a special feature of Llangollen life — and a wonderful excuse for dressing-up! Elaborately decorated floats were a traditional attraction, upon the leading one of which the Queen and her court would ride. Some attempt was made during the 1970s to revive this once-popular custom but it somehow failed to achieve the attraction enjoyed in earlier years.

Another exceedingly popular annual event has always been the Vale of Llangollen Sheepdog Trials, held for over one hundred years in the beautiful setting of Plas yn Vivod Park, home of the Best family, and on their adjoining Tyn y Celyn land. The Vale

Decorated floats awaiting the Queen and her court, May Day 1935.

Centenary Trials, Sheepdog Society, 1985. LEFT TO RIGHT: Peter Walker, Vice-Chairman; John Bailey, Secretary; Bob Best, Chairman; Tom Owen, Treasurer.

of Llangollen Sheepdog Society was formed in 1885, born out of the open trails first organised by Mr. Lloyd Price of Rhiwlas, Bala where he organised his first event in 1873. Previously, his main interest had been in the breeding and training of shooting dogs, making this a quite new and, as it turned out, a successful venture for him. However, he chose not to make it an annual event but did encourage local farmers to hold trials of their own.

It was upon the removal of the Trials to Vivod, under the patronage of Captain Best, RN that the Society was formed and annual Trials held. During 1889 Queen Victoria spent several days at Pale, Llanderfel, the home of Henry Robertson, where Captain Best arranged a demonstration of working sheepdogs for her entertainment. Her Majesty, being much impressed, was pleased to consent to becoming Patron of the Society, an example which was followed by Queen Alexander and Queen Mary.

The primary object of the Society is to promote improvement in the breeding and training of sheepdogs and to encourage public interest in their handling and working. As a result of the great popularity and profitability of this event, the Society has been able to make generous donations to local charities. Highly successful Trials were held at Plas yn Vivod in 1985 in celebration of the centenary of the Society, but in recent years the Trials have transferred to their venue to Llandyn.

The Vivod family were also instrumental in providing Llangollen with a Cottage Hospital. In 1875 Mr. William Wagstaff conveyed the land upon which the Hospital now

Staff and managers at Llangollen Hospital.

stands to the Local Board for the district of Llangollen. He had purchased it the previous year for this purpose and he had buildings erected on it "suitable for the reception of sick persons". Furthermore, he and a number of friends gave sufficient monies to the hospital trustees to form the nucleus of an endowment fund. The terms of the agreement allowed the arrangement to be "forever or so long as the premises should be kept up and used as a hospital".

However, if for any reason the Hospital should cease to function for "a period of six calendar months then this Conveyance should cease in its operation and the premises shall revert to the Donor and his heirs as of his old estate and interest therein".

The hospital was officially opened in April 1875, there having been nineteen patients admitted within the first year. Persons suffering from infections or incurable diseases were not admitted and each paid according to their means. The minimum weekly charge was two shillings and sixpence.

Mr. Wagstaff died in 1877 and the Vivod estate then passed to his daughter and her husband Captain Best, RN, whom she had married in April 1873. The family generously continued to head the list of voluntary contributors upon whom the hospital was dependent for its existence until it was taken over by the Minister of Health in 1947.

The 70th, and almost last, *Annual Report* (1945) finds the Best family still leading the list of subscribers with a combined donation of twenty guineas. Total receipts amounted to one thousand, three hundred and sixty seven pounds, ten shillings and ninepence, of which it is interesting to note that tenants of the Vivod estate contributed a total of one hundred and forty eight pounds, eleven shillings and sixpence. Of this Mr. J. Thomas, Cilmedw, had contributed one pound, seven shillings and sixpence. The rest gave either five shillings or half a crown.

Practical contributions were also received, examples being "Captain W. Best — Potatoes, plants, Strawberries, Rabbits, tomatoes and lettuces, Mr. Williams Fair View —

load of manure, Miss Jagger — Cauliflower, lettuces, flowers and a Duo-Ray lamp".

During 1945 one hundred and twenty patients had been admitted and a total of thirty-nine babies had been born within the hospital. Today, the hospital plays a valuable part in the community and has continued to grow while others elsewhere have ceased to exist. This has been achieved with the help of many people within the area and a dedicated Society of Friends.

Llangollen has a modern Health Centre housed in the former Church School. This was converted in 1986 to its current use at an estimated cost of a quarter of a million pounds. Surgeries had previously been housed in the now demolished Minfordd, situated at the foot of Wharf Hill and traditionally a doctor's residence for many years.

Before the First World War a quite remarkable young lady of Anglo-Scottish descent came to live in Llangollen, her father having taken the old house of Cwm Alis about two miles east of the town to provide a home for his children — Emma, Bertha, Helen and Arthur. Bertha was a talented artist and etcher who was able to make a living from her work, sold through the agency of Phillipson and Golder Ltd. of Frodsham Street, Chester. Her father had converted part of the coach house and stables building at Cwm Alis into a large and comfortable studio which she would be pleased to know is still used by the wife of the present owners.

In about 1913 she married Mr. John Aiken, son of Doctor Aiken of Llandrillo, physician and bacteriologist. John Aiken was a wealthy man — Director of Brymbo Steelworks and builder of the large house, Abbey Dingle, Llangollen. Here he added, for his bride, a large and airy studio as well as allowing her to gratify her many tastes and indulge without let and hindrance in numerous good works. She was fearless and outspoken in the cause of women's rights, founding the Women's Institutes in both Llangollen and her local village of Pentredwr, as well as being President for many years of the area branch of the National Council of Women.

1928 saw the realisation of a dream, when in June of that year Dame Agnes Hunt officially opened the newly built Welfare House. Not only had Mrs Aiken paid the entire cost of the building, but she had also designed it, inside and out, down to the very last detail. Upon completion it was rented to the County Medical Services at a peppercorn rent, to be used for maternity and child welfare, etc., as well as being placed at the disposal of the Girl Guides for a meeting place. The attractive building included an assembly hall, twenty by thirty feet, with platform and fireplace, consulting room, eye-testing facilities, dentist's room, kitchen and lavatory. Previously, eye-testing had been carried out on the Town Hall stage — "possibly the only dark place in Llangollen", Mrs Aiken had joked.

The opening celebrations covered a period of three days and were very well attended. Thursday 21st June saw the opening ceremony at 3.00 p.m., after which visitors could either take tea in the Scout House next door, patronise the gift stall in the Main Hall or visit the Model Child Welfare Exhibition in the adjoining Liberal Club. There was also a basket-making demonstration, country dancing display, soft-toy making demonstration and a Lantern Lecture entitled 'Sunlight Cure'.

Friday 22nd June offered pretty much the same as the previous day plus an evening play presented by Pentredwr Women's Institute entitled 'The Bakehouse'. Saturday 23rd included the previously-mentioned exhibitions and a demonstration of leather work, plus, the 'Annual Tea for Welfare Mothers' and in the early evening 'Children's Health Rhymes' by children from the Llangollen Welfare Centre, led by Miss Bessie Parry. The final item was a play by the Llangollen Snowdrop Band entitled 'Ail Ddechreu'.

The Welfare House, and the facilities it provided, proved to be an example many larger towns were to eventually follow. The building still stands unaltered in Market Street

Part of the interior of Welfare House.

and continues to be of great benefit to the town.

Mrs Aiken died in January 1938 from cancer of the throat — the knowledge of which she had kept from even her close friends. She had presided as usual at a committee meeting on 15th November at which she had undertaken to organise competitions at a Christmas party to be held on 9th December. It was only upon receipt of a message from her husband, stating that she was too unwell to attend, that it became apparent that all was not as it should be. Very sadly, she died almost within the month.

After her death Mr. John Aiken vested the freehold building and its contents in fifteen trustees — all women of course. At the official opening of the Welfare House in 1928, the vote of thanks had, according to the *Llangollen Advertiser*, "been proposed in eulogistic terms by Mr. Hiram Davies, the local representative on the Denbighshire County Council". This was seconded by Mr. Arthur Price, ex-Chairman of the Llangollen Urban District Council, with these words:

"There were people who had their doubts about the wisdom of extending the franchise to women, but these doubts, so far as Llangollen is concerned, have been removed in my mind after seeing the wonderful work that has been done here."

A little patronising perhaps, especially when one is certain that Bertha Gorst Aiken would have achieved her goals with or without the benefit of the franchise!

Welfare House, with all its comforts, is a long way removed from the old Llangollen Workhouse, which was built in 1786 at a cost of £200. As was often usual with such institutions, it stood a little away from, and in this case, above the town, being situated at the (now) junction of Vicarage Road and Fron Bache. The building has since been converted to two houses, Glenwood and Bryntirion.

Workhouses were not of necessity the grim places of incarceration as depicted by Charles Dickens, but most certainly were the last resort of the chronic poor and aged sick, unfortunate enough to lack the support of caring relations. It is difficult to see the alternative for those of us in a similar position today!

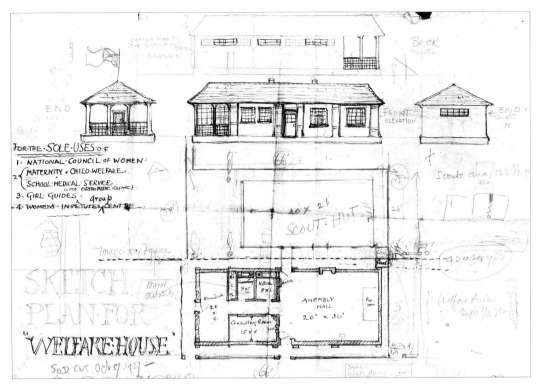

Original plans for the Welfare House drawn by Mrs. Aiken's own hand.

An earlier mention of Mr. J. Hiram Davies — all his life a long way from the workhouse — prompts a mention of the Llangollen Fire Brigade, of which he was the first Captain after its formation in 1901. Mr. Davies had long seen the need for an organised fire-fighting force armed with efficient equipment. Previously, the best he had been able to do was to provide a handcart, bearing forty-foot extending ladder, buckets and hose. This had to serve from 1864–1900 when it proved to be grossly ineffective at the great fire which destroyed Cowards' Timber Yard (now the site of a supermarket) in Regent Street. Clearly something had to be done.

The Fire Brigade consisted of ten men and two officers, all engaged on a part-time basis and paid an annual fee of one guinea. They were provided with a horse-drawn 'engine' complete with a steam-driven pump for the hose, the pressure for which was built up by means of a fire heated with coals. Fires within the area covered by the Llangollen District Council were attended free of charge while outbreaks attended in the outlying districts were charged individually as decided by the Brigade Committee.

The first Fire Station was erected in Market Street at one of the entrances to the Smithfield Market, the horses being housed in stables at the rear of the Bull Inn.

In the early 1960s it was decided to build a new fire station with up-to-date facilities in a position where easier exit facilities could be provided. Two sites were considered, one in Parade Street, which would not have provided better ease of exit. The other was Fair View Field (later the site of Jones Brothers short-lived petrol station, demolished to provide housing for the elderly). This, being on Abbey Road, posed the problem of regularly having to cross the narrow river Bridge. Eventually it was decided to employ the present Queen Street site, which necessitated the demolition of several properties to

Llangollen Fire Brigade annual picnic (possibly to Rhyl) 16th July 1914. Mr. Hiram Davies is seated in the centre of the front row.

provide the required amount of frontage. Now, in the event of a call-out, modern fire appliances with their powerful engines can be on the way in a matter of minutes. In the early days horsepower meant exactly that! And horses are only human — so to speak. There are reports of their having bolted on the way to attend a fire and on one occasion, even dropping dead! Sometimes they were not to be found at all.

In June 1919, there was the embarrassing situation as reported by the *Llangollen Advertiser* on Friday 13th of that month:

"Fire Alarm — Another fire alarm was rung in the town on Monday afternoon, when the Brigade were called to a fire at Chirk. The fire station was immediately besieged with crowds of visitors eager to see the turn-out, but after waiting a considerable time they were disappointed when it became known that no horses were available for the engine, and consequently the brigade could not proceed to the scene of the fire."

The following July we find the Fire Brigade committee resolving that:

"... inquiries be made as to what conditions army horses could be obtained and that for the present two horses from Mr. F. Evans be retrained for the engine. The committee further recommended that Mr. E. H. Lloyd be asked to place his motor van at the disposal of the Fire Brigade if required."

All in all we have come a long way since then and the even earlier days of the hand-cart, ladder and buckets — no doubt long since snapped up by some enterprising window-cleaner!

Plas Newydd (Pen-y-Maes) as the Ladies first saw it. From an 18th century print. Artist unknown.

𝒫𝓁𝒶𝓈 𝒩𝑒𝓌𝓎𝒹𝒹 𝒶𝓃𝒹 𝓉𝒽𝑒 𝓛𝒶𝒹𝒾𝑒𝓈

The story of the 'Ladies of Llangollen' and their unique home could fill a book — and has, more than one — but can only be briefly dealt with here. Their arrival in Llangollen was almost accidental, but having decided to settle here the impact they made upon an insignificant Welsh town was more than considerable.

Lady Eleanor Charlotte Butler and Miss Sarah Ponsonby were members of two of the foremost families of the Anglo-Irish aristocracy. One was the youngest daughter of Walter Butler, head of the Roman Catholic branch of the Ormonde family, and sister of John Butler, 17th Earl of Ormonde. The other was an orphan granddaughter of General Henry Ponsonby and second cousin to the third Earl of Besborough. Eleanor and Sarah first met when the latter was at boarding school near Kilkenny, while Eleanor lived close by at Kilkenny Castle. Both were unhappy at home. Eleanor was under much pressure from her mother to make an advantageous marriage or enter a convent and Sarah was troubled by the very unwelcome attentions of her guardian, Sir William Fownes.

In March 1778 the pair, who had become close friends, decided to run away together disguised in men's clothing. But their plan was thwarted — they were seized at

Waterford and returned to their respective homes. They were more successful in May of the same year when they sailed from Ireland to Milford Haven. From there they toured Pembrokeshire, travelling north via Machynlleth arriving in Oswestry on 25th May before moving on from there to Llangollen. Here they spent the night, rising early the following morning to climb Dinas Brân and the Trevor Rocks, later visiting the Abbey and finally walking to Chirk Castle! Such energy, but Sarah was a mere twenty-three against Eleanor's thirty-nine years.

By the end of the month they were in Conwy, moving on to spend a month in Caernarfonshire, but were back in Oswestry for the end of June. Wishing to find a place to put up for the winter they returned to Llangollen, lodging first at Blaen Bache and then with John Jones at the Post Office. From here they were successful in obtaining the tenancy of Pen y Maes, a small stone cottage above the town, in the ownership of Edward Edwards of Pengwern Vale. Having taken possession of the house during the month of May 1780, the Ladies remained there for half a century. That is, until their deaths in 1829 and 1831.

After taking a ninety-nine year lease on the house, the Ladies set about making it their home, building the library and the state bedroom above. Laying out and ornamenting the grounds with bower, summerhouse and ornamental bridges astride the rushing River Cyflymen. Also, they established the tradition of adding carved oak decoration to the once plain building, which they had re-named Plas Newydd.

A rare porcelain 'nodding' figure of Mary Carryl from the author's collection.

In 1819 their landlord, "that venerable man", having died, his son John Edwards sold Plas Newydd to the Ladies but it was not until 1825 that they were able to finish paying for it. Additional land amounting to some two-and-a-half acres was rented from the Reverend Edward Roberts of Dinbren Hall. Upon his death in 1805 their faithful friend and housekeeper Mary Carryl purchased the land known as Aberadda from his executors. The name recalls that of Adda of Pengwern who married Isabel, sister to Owain Glyndwr.

Mary Carryl had been employed as a maid at the time of Sarah's 'escape' in which she aided and abetted. Dismissed for throwing a candlestick at a fellow servant and known thereafter as 'Molly the Bruiser', she followed Sarah and Eleanor just as soon as they had settled in Llangollen. Dignified with the prefix 'Mrs.' before her name, Mary devoted her life to looking after the best interests of the household — seeing-off tramps and bargaining with the tradesmen. In her will — witnessed by Richard Jones, Grocer and known admirer — she left the Aberadda fields and her life savings (amounting to some £350) to Miss Ponsonby. The grateful Ladies planted an avenue of lime and beech in her memory.

One must assume the enduring fame of the

Ladies to lie in what was considered to be their eccentricity. Preferring always to dress in dark riding habits with white starched neck cloths, their cropped and powdered hair surmounted by tall black beaver hats gave them a distinctive, almost masculine, appearance. Lady Eleanor, the elder, was a veracious but interesting talker — as Chief Justice Charles Dendal Bushe confirmed in a letter to his wife written after a visit in September 1805:

> *"They gave me all the news of Dublin, London, Cheltenham, Paris and everywhere in a moment; everything that they said (I should have said SHE, for Miss Ponsonby is but an accompanist) was pointed, naïve, polished and interesting — sometimes satirical always witty."*

Their visitors were numerous and famous. The Duke of Gloucester, nephew of George the III, dined there in 1809. Prince Paul Esterhazy and his wife came to breakfast as the result of a letter of introduction from the Duke of Wellington. The Duke himself first called in 1788, as plain Arthur Wellesley, and was thought to be a "charming young man, handsome, tall and elegant", who was to be received on several subsequent occasions

Sir Walter Scott was, in retrospect, better thought of than the poet Wordsworth who, with his family, took tea with the Ladies in 1824. Afterwards, he sent them a poem composed in the grounds. Unfortunately his referring to their beloved Plas Newydd as a "low roofed cot" failed to amuse them and he was not invited to call again!

Local callers included Sir Watkin Williams Wynn, Wynnstay; Lady Dungannon, Brynkinallt; The Ormesbys and the Gores (Lord Harlech's ancestors); The Myddletons of Chirk Castle; together with Shannette the Witch; Jonathon Hughes, with a translation of his Eisteddfodic ode; and little Pryce "to show his new green coat".

There is a long-held belief that the Ladies slept not one night away from their house, preferring instead to rise early when visiting far-away friends and often not returning until the early hours of the following day. For such journeys they would hire a carriage from the Hand Inn or, on such occasions as that establishment was out of favour, the Lyon would be used instead. In order to keep the belief intact, we will not mention their three-day visit to Barmouth with Miss Bowlder, which surely would have necessitated their occupying a strange bed!

Walking in the lovely local countryside was another great pleasure, favourite excursions being to the Abbey and Dinbren.

Not only did they get their butter, lard and turkeys from Dinbren Isaf, but they also had great friends in the Reverend and Mrs. Roberts at the Hall. One suspects it to have been this friendship that led them to worship at Llantysilio Church for a period, even though they had often to wait for the Vicar a long time. "We sat three quarters of an hour in the Church porch" recorded Lady Eleanor on one occasion. Small wonder, for Mr. Roberts was also Rector of Llansantffraid, Glynceiriog as well as being perpetual curate of Llantysilio. It is most certainly a long trek from one to the other!

The Ladies steadfastly refused to sit for their portraits, which may seem surprising when one considers the large number of seemingly authentic prints, post cards and even figurines which are offered for sale. The answer is that all these were based upon the sketch, obtained by stratagem, by Mary Parker of Sweeney Hall, Shropshire who was a talented amateur artist. In the company of the Honourable Mrs. Kenyon of Pradoe she paid a call upon the Ladies. Lady Eleanor, by now old and suffering from failing eyesight, was kept in engaging, lively conversation by Mrs. Kenyon, while Mary Parker,

The Mary Parker painting.

under the pretence of copying a piece of music, sketched their likeness on a drawing block balanced on her knee below the rim of the library table around which they were all sitting. Such details as the objects upon the table and general room furnishings were added later.

From this painting, later reproduced in quantity from the engraving made by R.J. Lane, ARA, sprang all the other so-called 'authentic' paintings showing the Ladies in their garden, by the ancient font and even on horseback. The artist simply painted whatever he or she felt would sell and 'borrowed' the features from Mary Parker's work. All these are quite spurious and most certainly did not appear before the Ladies' deaths.

Another watercolour by Lady Henrietta Delamere, daughter of Sir Watkin Williams Wynn showing them walking in the library, was painted in 1828 possibly from memory, and as far as one knows has not been reproduced.

A miniature of the young Sarah Ponsonby is reproduced in the Hamwood Papers and a portrait of a lady, looking rather more like Eleanor Butler than Sarah Ponsonby (whom it is reputed to be), in a tall hat, seated with flute, now hangs in Plas Newydd. It was formerly the property of Miss Sara Pugh Jones and is to hang in the house in accordance with the conditions of her will. Both the Mary Parker and Lady Delamere paintings are also to be seen there.

In 1977 Christies of London offered for sale by public auction a large portrait of Lady Eleanor in which she had the appearance of being about sixty years old. The portrait, sold without provenance, was purchased by the late Miss Pugh Jones and is now in the ownership of a member of the Butler family, whose husband had Llangollen roots.

In the glen showing the Ladies' font from Valle Crucis Abbey.

Curiously, Miss Pugh Jones, an expert on the history of Plas Newydd and the Ladies, never found Eleanor's portrait comfortable to live with.

Eleanor was a particularly enthusiastic correspondent and devoted much of her time to the keeping of her journal. It is interesting to record that letters of the day were addressed thus:

"To Miss Butler, Llangollen, Salop Post, Oswestry Bag, North Wales."

No post code! One such letter received obviously failed to please, and prompted the following entry in her journal:

"Monday, June 29th — Letter from Lady Dungannon. Like everything she does, ungrateful and disagreeable!"

Poor Lady Dungannon, to whom they were often indebted for gifts of game etc., and with whom they would regularly meet to play cards. Perhaps Eleanor had lost heavily. The journal too, gives a useful insight into travel times and conditions of the day:

"Saturday, August 16th at half-past seven went in the Hand Chaise to Halston. Met a multitude of wagons, coal carts, one caravan — a young couple in it who appeared innocent and interesting. Arrived at Halston precisely at nine. Mrs. and Miss Mytton in the beautiful parlour."

Halston Hall lies on the Ellesmere Road as one leaves Whittington and the journey there took one-and-a-half hours. Today, the same distance could easily be accomplished in half an hour at most.

Although the Ladies came to Llangollen in order to lead quiet lives in a romantic, rustic retirement, there have always been those determined to credit them with other motives — after their deaths, of course!

The *Morning Post*, obviously short of copy resulting in a slow news day in 1910 (month unknown), once decided to devote almost a full column to them. Under the pretence of drawing attention to the forthcoming sale of Plas Newydd and its contents — of which the paper somehow forgot to give any details — the writer, 'E.G.R.', attempts to build a case against the Ladies, whom he suggests were probably government agents. True, they were in receipt of a civil list pension but:

"Why? The reader may well ask. What claim had two eccentric spinsters on the government during all these years? A definite answer may never be forthcoming, but when one remembers how carefully they planted themselves on the broad highway between England and Ireland, in the years immediately proceeding the Union; how they encouraged the visits of Politicians, and of foreign visitors; how they wrote long letters to and received long letters from, men who were certainly in the secrets of courts and cabinets and politician parties; how their home, once again for sale, was a nest of hiding-places; and how, lastly, it was found that their vast correspondence had almost entirely disappeared after their deaths — one arrives at the conclusion that the payments and pensions mentioned were nothing more than compensation for services rendered of which the government of the day was only too ready to avail themselves."

And this was only half of the concluding paragraph! E.G.R. was obviously not familiar with the house or its history, or he would have known that the much enlarged Plas Newydd referred to earlier in the article was the work of later owners. As was the "china cupboard — really a door leading to another set of apartments", and a "clothes press with a false back which lead into an inner room".

Later on, other stories were put about including the famous myth that the Ladies had had the tower built in the grounds in order to spy upon comings and goings along the Holyhead Road with the aid of a large brass telescope. Interesting — especially when one considers that the building was erected by a much later owner to serve as a water tower!

The notorious Colette in her book *Ces Plaisirs* speculated upon another aspect of their lives. She extracts from Lady Eleanor's journal such entries as she felt would suit her theories, writing:

"Can we possibly imagine the Ladies of Llangollen in this year of 1930? They would own a car, wear dungarees, smoke cigarettes, have short hair, and there would be a bar in their apartment. Would Sarah Ponsonby still know how to remain silent? Perhaps with the aid of crossword puzzles. Eleanor Butler would curse as she jacked up the car and would have her breasts amputated."

It is always pleasurable to stumble across a well-written and erudite volume! It took thirty-six years for the book to appear in Britain in translation and under the title *The Pure and the Impure*. Not surprisingly, a North Wales weekly newspaper seized upon the passage concerning the Ladies and attempted to work it up into an ongoing sensational series of articles. But the whole thing fell flat — no one really cared.

Lady Eleanor Butler died in June 1829 and was followed in December 1831 by her grieving companion. They are, together with their faithful Mary Carryl, buried in Llangollen Churchyard. Both are now permanently sleeping away from home.

Plas Newydd did not remain empty for long, being purchased — one suspects

Plas Newydd at the time of the 'Lollies and the Trollies'.

gleefully — by another two spinster ladies Amelia Lolley and Charlotte Andrew. These two had lived in Llangollen for some time and had a reputation for attempting to emulate the Ladies' way of life. Lady Eleanor was known to refer to them as the "Lollies and the Trollies" and would most certainly not have seen them as worthy successors. Having placed a large, stuffed bear in the porch, they went on to 'ornament' the grounds with curious wooden objects. One contemporary visitor considered the "whole place had a vulgar and commonplace appearance". By 1861 they were both dead and gone, the estate passing to Mrs. Robina Augusta Couran of Plympton, Devon, who held it for fifteen years before selling to Richard Lloyd Williams of Denbigh.

It may be that Mr. Lloyd Williams purchased the estate purely as a speculative investment, for within months he had sold it on to General John Yorke of London, a member of the Erddig family and companion of the Order of the Bath. For the remainder of his life, General Yorke made Plas Newydd his chief pursuit, building the extensive west wing and opening the older rooms to the public. He made the grounds a paradise for birds, squirrels and peacocks as well as developing the Hermitage site.

General Yorke died in 1890 whereupon his heir, Colonel Reynoldson, sold the property to two brothers — H.R. and G.H.F. Robertson of Liverpool. The latter of these came to reside there with his family, making it a delightful home.

Together with their Head Gardener, Mr. Mossop, they laid out the formal gardens, adding a topiary and a shrubbery. A not altogether successful service wing was added to the original frontage, this having been largely prefabricated in the workshops of

The wedding of Miss Robertson, Plas Newydd. Date unknown.

Messrs. Bolton and Paul. In their turn the Robertson brothers, whom it must be stressed were in no way related to Henry Robertson of railway fame, sold the estate to Mrs. G.M. Wilson of Lincoln who took up residence but about whom little is known. In 1918, after eight years of ownership, Mrs. Wilson sold to Mr. G. Harrison of Bryntysilio — again a mysterious purchaser for he neither needed nor occupied the property, simply selling it on within the year to J.H. Duveen, a well-known dealer in antiques.

Lord Duveen, as he became in 1927, was thought to have bought Plas Newydd for its wealth of carved oak, much of it ancient and likely to make a good price in the right market. This was almost certainly in his mind. However, he mercifully changed his mind at the last, possible feeling that the exercise was not financially viable. So the house was spared, being sold three months later to the Rt. Honourable George Montague, 7th Earl of Tankerville.

Lord Tankerville died in 1931 but his widow continued to use Plas Newydd as a summer residence, her eldest son and his bride spending their honeymoon there. In November 1932 the contents of the house were sold by public auction and negotiations began with Llangollen Urban District Council, who had acquired

General Yorke's West Wing.

the property in March 1933.

Once more the old rooms of the Ladies' house were opened to public gaze and the west wing became the home of the Welsh National Theatre, under the patronage of Lord Howard de Walden, at that time the tenant of Chirk Castle.

The Welsh National Theatre Company Ltd. was established on 7th July 1933, with Lord Howard de Walden as Chairman, at the Arts Theatre Club, London. Richard Hughes was appointed Vice-Chairman, Evelyn Bowen Secretary, and W.S. Gwynne Williams as Music Director. Only four months previously, Llangollen Urban District Council had purchased Plas Newydd and Lord Howard lost no time in securing a lease on the west wing. In the late summer Evelyn Bowen arrived, accompanied by her large black dog, and the first of the local help was provided in the person of Mrs. Gladys Pugh who took up the post of housekeeper. She presided over the kitchen and seeing to the creature comforts of the company throughout the six years they were based there. Mrs. Nesta Hannaby came as seamstress for the costumes which were designed by Bruce Winston.

During the month of April 1934, the company performed their first two plays in Llangollen Town Hall — *Y Gainc Olaf*, especially

Mrs. Gladys Pugh in the room in which Richard Llewelyn wrote 'How Green Was My Valley'.

written by T. Gwynn Jones and W.S. Gwynn Williams, and *Howell of Gwent* by J.O. Francis. Afterwards, the company began a tour of Wales which began at Llanarmon, reaching Cardiff in time for Christmas where they performed the *Story of Bethlehem* to packed houses. The proceeds were given to the Gresford Colliery Disaster Fund.

Having become very successful, the company was called upon to perform outside Wales. They gave memorable performances in both English and Welsh in Liverpool — which had a strong Welsh population and was often referred to as the capital of North Wales — and also crossing the Channel at the invitation of the Paris Welsh Society! Certain proof of the old saying that when two or three Welshmen are gathered together, they will immediately form a committee.

The famous writer Emlyn Williams was one of the three official advisers to the Welsh National Theatre and the company gave a chilling performance of his gripping *Night Must Fall*. Several

Flyer for a Welsh National Theatre production.

Former members of the Welsh National Theatre Company at the pre-demolition party in 1963.

open-air performances were given in the romantic setting of Valle Crucis, the cast being made up of many local people. Perhaps the most memorable of these being *Llwyfan y Byd*, with special lighting effects managed by Lord Howard de Walden, during which three angels appeared, one in each lancet of the east window, a scene most vividly remembered. The cast list reveals that one of the angels was played by 'Annie Glynne Jones', still a familiar figure in the town.

The company's first 'Annual School of Dramatic Art' was held from the 18th–25th May 1934 at Plas Newydd, with crowds of aspiring young actors descending upon Llangollen in the hope of being taken on. Richard Llewelyn came up from South Wales to audition them and took such a liking to the place that he stayed on for several months, occupying a small room between the west wing and the main building. It was here that he wrote, *How Green Was My Valley*, sustained by countless cups of tea brought up by the invaluable Gladys Pugh. Mrs. Pugh remembered him as a 'dandy' with a huge wardrobe of suits, shoes and ties for every possible occasion. Richard Llewelyn gave her a beautiful photograph of his sister, later sadly killed by a landmine in London's Green Park during the early years of the Second World War.

And the war it was which put an end to the Welsh National Theatre. The company, performing in Paris in 1939 on the outbreak of the War, had to hurriedly vacate the country leaving their props and valuable costumes behind. Back at home they toured England, Scotland and Wales with their production of *Pygmalion* as part of ENSA, the organisation responsible for entertaining troops in training camps. Soon afterwards the time came for male actors to be called up and so ended the short life of the theatre.

In 1963 the Urban District Council decided, in their wisdom, to demolish both the west and east wings of Plas Newydd leaving the house more or less as it was at the time of the Ladies. The west wing was a particularly sad loss and could have served the town well in many capacities had it been allowed to survive. Since the departure of the National Theatre it had been leased to the Broadhurst family as a private residence, the east wing being occupied by the caretaker and his family.

However, a 'pre-demolition party' was allowed to be held, giving the people of Llangollen the opportunity to say their farewells to this unique building — the party being held in the now empty west wing. People came from far and wide, many being connected with the theatre together with others who included representatives of the Mossop family.

On the 19th June 1963 Jackson-Stops & Staff of Chester held the pre-demolition sale — on the premises, of course. The catalogue consisted of ten poorly duplicated sheets, stapled together in the top left-hand corner. Quite obviously, it had not been thought desirable to go to the expense of a better production. The cost of it was only one shilling and it served also as a permit to view. Lot 1 was a "W.C. pedestal, cast iron cistern, linking pipe" which was hardly an auspicious start and somehow set the tone for the sale. Although very well attended, lots were 'given away' — the prices realised being quite unbelievable, especially by today's standards.

Among the ten secured by the writer was lot 129 — "Approximately 65 sq. ft. carved apsi-form panelling including small corner cupboard with carved door" — secured for the maiden bid of one pound! This panelling had clothed the walls of the haunted bedroom and was reassembled in a room in the purchaser's home. The ghost did not come with it — possibly too much to hope for such small expenditure.

The much-reduced Plas Newydd of today.

Chirk Castle, the influence of which was long-felt in Llangollen.

Historic Houses & Estates

It is to be remembered that homesteads, and not towns, are the basis of Welsh life and it is therefore necessary to look into the surrounding countryside to find the more ancient of the larger houses. Plas Pengwern was, of course, one of these as is Llangollen Fechan, now much altered and used as a private nursing home. In so many cases the first impression given as one approaches is often of a much later building, as changing styles and a desire to be fashionable led the owner, were he wealthy enough, to 'keep up with the Joneses'.

Rebuilding upon the same site was not unknown but more often, in these parts, it was a question of doing the best with what one had. New windows were, as today, so often the first step, accompanied by an updating of the door case and porch area. Rooflines were raised, often by the addition of an extra storey, to accommodate a further servant or two but mostly to impress the visitor or passer by. Venture around the side or into the backyard and one would find the old house still intact. Truly a case of Queen Anne fronts with Mary Ann backs!

Inside might be found a new staircase and, almost certainly, fashionable chimney pieces, although funds might dictate, especially in the 18th century, that carved and decorative marble be copied in wood — normally painted pine. Give-away signs included the height and dimensions of rooms, often necessitating the modern alterations to be constructed out of scale. Were one allowed a glimpse beyond the entertaining rooms we might at once, step back a century or so. Llangollen Fechan, for many generations, home of the Hughes-Parry family, was a charming example of such a dwelling.

Llangollen Fechan, c.1912.

The Manor House of Plas Uchaf, Eglwyseg is without doubt the finest local example of an ancient house. It has survived largely intact. Built on the site of an earlier dwelling, the place is much involved with the history of early 12th century Wales. It was here, legend has it, that Owain son of Cadwgan Prince of Powys brought the beautiful Nest, whom he had abducted from her husband Gerald de Windsor of Pembroke in about 1109.

Of the House as it is at present, dating from the Tudor and Elizabethan periods, the most interesting ownership was that of Colonel John Jones — later known as the Regicide. He married Margaret Evans of Stansty, Plas Uchaf being their home when not in London or Dublin, of which Cromwell had made him Commander. It was in Dublin that Margaret died and three years later John Jones was re-married to Cromwell's widowed sister. A fine portrait of Oliver Cromwell as painted by Lely hung in this house until about 1900.

It is said that Colonel Jones, knowing that his doom was pending after the return of Charles II, left his refuge at the home of friends, stealing by night to Plas Uchaf to spend a brief time in the home he had loved and spent his happiest years. A facsimile of John Jones's signature on Charles I's death warrant may be seen at Plas Newydd and it is therefore understandable that he was not popular with Charles II. He was arrested and executed, Samuel Pepys recording his encounter in a London street with the Colonel's still-smoking limbs.

Thomas Jones (1819–94) of Plas Llanerchrugog, who would appear to have been a person of romantic tastes, purchased Plas Uchaf. He took a great interest in its history

Thomas Jones from an original portrait (in the author's collection).

and upkeep. It was he who was responsible for the inscribed stones (now lost) above the front door, which gave a short list of the Kings of Wales so far back in the mists of time as to make them incontrovertible. It seems that their fate was mostly to be 'slain in battle'. Above these was a fine tablet displaying the arms of Jones of Llanerchrugog — a rampant lion upon a crested shield, over which a dragon, to the left, the sun in strength balanced to the right by a griffin. The motto, *Ovner Na Ovno Angau* (fear him who fears not death), was very sound advice!

Thomas Jones married Miss Raikes, sister to the H.M. Postmaster General, and spent so much money at the manor house that upon his death in 1894 the estate was found to be heavily mortgaged. Curiously, in his will the Plas Uchaf estate was bequeathed to the widow of his physician, who being mindful of the financial implications, soon parted with it to Sir Watkin Williams Wynn.

It was about this time that the indefatigable Fletcher Moss, in the company of his faithful friend the photographer 'X', visited Plas Uchaf after a long and difficult journey. Here they found another Nest in residence as caretaker/housekeeper who had, it transpired, as much English as they had Welsh. This made conversation exceedingly difficult. Furthermore, it became apparent that she did not care for foreigners, especially those staggering beneath curious tripodic devices, but was eventually persuaded, no doubt by the glint of coin, to let them into the house. Here they were shown the bed of Prince Llewelyn, "A very ancient bedstead, made of massive oaken boards, bound together with ropes, and shaped like a big cradle with a wooden hood over the head".

The Lely portrait of Oliver Cromwell had been recently removed for reasons of safety, having being deemed too valuable to be left, but one of his mother by the same artist was still to be seen. There was also another portrait, said to be a very fine one, of an eighty-three year old man, which was dated 1628. Sitter and artist unknown.

Fletcher Moss described the interior thus:

"There is an oaken staircase, oaken rafters, oaken panelling. Chairs that were made to last for ages, not to sell. Weapons of war, trophies of the chase, but where are the instruments of music, for this should have been a place for the inspiration of the bards? Its glamour steals over us as the daylight dies. The diamond paned windows are deeply set, the trees above cast greyish flickering shadows on the walls, while the giant hills encircle and look down on all. It is indeed a ghostly place. Does the fair Nest come again to see the home of her captivity? Does reckless Owen moan for the delusive joys he ne'er shall have again."

How one longs to have been able to see it then!

In the summer of 1941 incendiary bombs fell on the roof of the manor house during two nights when the whole Eglwyseg moorland was a blaze of fire from the same cause. For the remainder of the war years the Army and forestry workers occupied the house. Its consequent dilapidation's were only repaired when Mr. Anthony Jones of Llangollen acquired it from the Wynnstay estate. The fine oaken staircase and panelling were gone and much needed to be done in order to make it habitable again.

About this time the little valley, previously a *cul de sac*, was opened up by the building of a new road over the mountain to Minera — now a favourite tourist route — which robbed Plas Uchaf of its romantic seclusion.

Following the death of Mr. Anthony Jones the house was uninhabited for several years, falling in to a state of decay. Its boarded windows and neglected roof presenting

The Manor House today.

a dismal sight until it was purchased by the present owners, Mr. and Mrs. Guy Kennaway. Their extensive and expert restoration has been the salvation of the house. Also, the re-routing of the public road (at the Kennaway's expense) has once more restored a sense of privacy to the property and provided a setting worthy of so fine a home.

Plas Yn Pentre during its restoration. (Photograph: Ron Thomson.)

Plas yn Pentre was originally a grange for Valle Crucis Abbey. The present ancient house is, at the time of writing, enjoying loving restoration at the hands of its owners. For a long time part of the Argoed Hall estate, the then sitting tenant Mr. Roy Bailey bought the property. Mr. Bailey successfully farmed the surrounding acres for many years before retiring to Chirk.

Following his retirement several successive owners made what they saw to be their own improvements, but it has taken the courage of the present family to remove the stucco-cladding which had for so long covered all but the attic storey. The impressive timber-framed, three gable front with narrow cross wings is now revealed as it was originally designed and once again makes good architectural sense. The semi-Venetian sash windows as shown in the photograph date from perhaps as late as 1820 and upon being replaced with those correct for the period, one will view the house pretty much as built in 1634.

During the days of religious persecution Plas yn Pentre enjoyed an exciting history, its priest's holes and secret passages being

Trevor Hall before the fire.

much used. Fragments of marble statuary dating from this period were later discovered in hiding places between the floors.

Close by is Ffynon Yryrog, a clear spring of very cold water reputed to possess healing powers, especially in cases of rheumatism and related conditions. Following the lane in the direction of Bryn Howell, Plas yn Pentre or Trevor Mill, a fine cut Cefn sandstone building dated 1848 is soon reached. The four-storey building has a low-pitched roof, which gives it quite a stylish appearance, and has also been the subject of sympathetic restoration. Although now a private dwelling, much of the original machinery remains, as does the large, over-shot mill wheel.

Trevor Hall, an eye-catching, mellow redbrick mansion, stands on a wooded hillside above the Llangollen to Wrexham Road, north of Plas yn Pentre. An excellent view of all these buildings can be had from the Holyhead Road on the other side of the valley.

Once the hub of a large and prosperous estate, Trevor Hall occupies an ancient site and was the home of Bishop John Trevor, builder of Llangollen Bridge. The Hall is one of a series of important North Wales houses built by various members of the powerful Trevor family of which only Brynkinallt a fine, largely Jacobean mansion near Chirk, remains directly within their ownership today.

The Hall at Trevor has an impressive façade of the George II period. Built in 1742 of handmade, wood-fired brick with handsome sandstone pedimented door-case, quoins and string courses, a close look at the side and rear elevations indicates that the south front is in fact a 'modernisation' of a much earlier house, formerly entirely of stone with leaded mullion windows. The interior was altered at the same time and a fine, full-height staircase was installed.

The house was sold away from the remains of the estate during the mid-1950s, after which it suffered a succession of owners, many of whom did little more than 'asset strip' before selling on.

January 1963 brought with it one of the harshest periods of winter weather the valley had known and the snow-bound mansion suffered a mysterious and disastrous fire in the early hours of one morning. The Fire Brigade, eventually alerted, found their work much hampered by the arctic conditions and the unavailability of mains water. The house was reduced to a smouldering shell.

Thus, for the second time in two years the future of this important building was under serious threat. On the first occasion the then owner had sought permission to demolish it in order to build several 'executive dwellings' on the site. The Local Authority raised no objections but the intervention of local people and an extensive public enquiry resulted in them deciding in favour of a preservation order being made. The house had been saved.

But what would happen next? Mercifully, it was decided that as the main walls had remained intact (apart from some sightless windows), as had the greater part of the principal staircase, the house should be allowed to stand in the hope of eventual restoration. Later, a temporary flat roof was fitted and some attempt made to keep the weather out. For the next twenty-five years the mansion stood as a forlorn ruin, serving only as a store for agricultural impedimenta and occasionally giving shelter to livestock.

In 1987 a Mr. Michael Tree, employed as a chartered surveyor by the Crown Estates in London, purchased the property after very protracted negotiations and embarked upon a mammoth programme of restoration. Because of the importance of the building, this costly work was assisted by grant aid totalling £431,000, thus allowing the house to be restored into a habitable condition. Eleven years later Michael Tree sold the property to Mr. Louis Parker, who has completed the restoration of the interior, erected outbuildings and established a new driveway — a more fitting access than the previous arrangement, which seemed to be never free of farmyard mire. Today, Trevor Hall is once again a much-loved family home. Sadly, within recent weeks, the untimely death of Mr. Louis Parker was announced.

Old Llantysilio Hall, once described as "a large brick building, bearing a strong affinity to Trevor Hall in antiquity of erection", sadly no longer stands but its site, up river from the Horseshoe Falls and the delightful little Church which nestles below the road, is still easily identified.

For many years a photograph of the old Hall, showing a handsome well-balanced brick house built in 1734, hung in the drawing room of the present mansion — also shown as in the course of erection and surrounded by scaffolding. The original builder, as far as can be discovered, was a Davies, of

Llantysilio Hall, c.1925.

whom there were, and are, many, but of this particular branch we know nothing except that the estate eventually passed through the female line to a family known as the 'Cuppers of the North'. Again, there being no male heir, the estate went to a daughter. She, having married Mr. Thomas Jones of Llanlloddian in Montgomeryshire, established the family of that name at Llantysilio.

Upon the death of the last of this line no will could be found and the estate passed into Chancery — to the consternation of several persons who had expectations. One of these caused the coffin of the dear departed to be illegally exhumed and opened, at dead of night, in the vain hope as seen in a dream that the will had been buried with the deceased. The last representative of the family to reside in the area was the late Major Stanley Douglas-Jones of Rhosynwst, Glyndyfrdwy who died in c.1971. By the 1820s we find the house in the possession of a Major Harrison who had finally been able to prove his case to inherit. After him came Mr. E. Wynne — of short tenure for by the mid-1840s the estate was in the hands of Alexander Reid Esquire.

Alexander Reid, it would seem, was a man of some means who had invested with Henry Robertson and others in Brymbo Ironworks as well as being a partner in lead mine workings at Minera. Later, he extended his business holdings to include the Llangollen Flagstone Company with slate quarries at Clogau, Moel y Faen, Oernant, Rhiw Goch and later Voel Vain.

After his death at the age of 73 on 28th February 1866 the Hall remained within the family until being offered for sale in September 1867. Charles Frederick Beyer, a bachelor and founder of Beyer Peacock and Company, locomotive builders, of Manchester then purchased the estate. Like Reid, he was a close friend of Henry Robertson and may well have known the place of old. Robertson had rendered financial assistance to Beyer when first setting up his business. Beyer did not forget this and some indication of the close relationship existing between the two may be illustrated by the Robertsons having christened their first born Henry Beyer Robertson with Charles Beyer standing as god-father.

In c.1873 Robertson decided to build the fine country mansion known as Pale, Llandrillo for his family. Beyer, being rather taken with the idea, followed suit and decided upon a site above the old Hall. First, he built the cellars but at ground level, later banking and levelling earth around them so as to form a great garden plateau. Both houses were built of fine Ashlar-stone from the same quarry and one can well see that two such successful businessmen would instinctively buy in bulk. It is also quite likely that the same master masons would have been employed and the high-quality ornamental carving, which adorns the exterior of both houses, would appear to be by the same hand.

Llantysilio was completed in 1874 to the design of the architect, F. Porteney-Smith, with much of the new furniture being designed and made especially for the house by the famous cabinetmakers Gillows of Lancaster. Very sadly, the old Hall was demolished in 1875. Curiously, Beyer chose to spend very little time at his new mansion, leaving it upon his death to his godson — Henry Beyer Robertson.

During the last War, and for some years afterwards, Llantysilio provided a home to 'Number Two House' of Morton Hall School. After the departure of the School, Mr. and Mrs. Duncan Robertson and their family took up residence. In recent years, following the death of Mr. Robertson, the house was sold away from the estate, which otherwise remains intact.

Bryntysilio, often described as an 'Italianate' residence, began life as a modest farmhouse romantically named Braich y Gwynt. The property had been purchased by Mr.

Richard Ellerton, who later moved across the valley, and it was from him that Sir Theodore and Lady Martin rented the house as a summer residence.

Sir Theodore had been born in Edinburgh in 1816 and had at first served as Parliamentary Agent for the family firm of Martin and Leslie, Abingdon Street, Westminster. Outside his professional work, he was much interested in literature and was the author of several major works and translations. For many years the Official Guide to Llangollen described him as "the intimate friend of Queen Victoria"! Mercifully, "intimate" was not at that time credited with today's connotation. Had it been, one feels her Majesty would certainly not have been amused and would no doubt have held from him the knighthood largely conferred for his having written the official biography of the Prince Consort.

In 1851 Theodore Martin married Helena Faucit, the well-known Shakespearean actress and youngest daughter of Saville Faucit, also an actor, as were five of his six children. Ten years later, Helena recorded in her journal:

"Summer and autumn were spent by us at Bryntysilio on the banks of the Dee about two miles above Llangollen. We were so charmed with the situation and the surrounding scenery that we resolved to buy the property if it ever came on the market. In 1865 the opportunity came, the house then only a cottage, and the adjoining grounds were bought."

Soon the work of enlarging the house began but progress was slow, which greatly displeased Helena as her journal entries revealed. It was late 1870 before all was completed to her satisfaction. Meanwhile, their London home at 31 Onslow Square hosted many grand dinner parties as their position within society became firmly established. In April 1868 Sir Theodore and Lady Martin had been invited by Queen Victoria to accompany her on a tour of Germany, thus cementing the firm friendship which was to last the remainder of their lives.

It therefore comes as no surprise to learn that the Queen was pleased to take tea at Bryntysilio during her official visit to Llangollen in 1889. Everything possible was done to make her feel 'at home', for in the entrance hall stood a bust of the young Victoria when eight years old, while the passage contained a statuette of Her Majesty which she had presented to Lady Martin. The drawing room, beautifully furnished in the Italian style, had as the principal adornment upon its walls a splendid silver plaque entitled 'Much Ado About Nothing' which had been presented to Sir Theodore by the Queen.

After a morning of miserable weather the sun eventually appeared in order to welcome Her Majesty, who arrived a little after four and was taken upstairs in order to fully appreciate the magnificent view over

Bryntisilio today.

the Horseshoe Falls to the hills beyond. Here too, she was shown Sir Theodore's dressing room in which he had written *The Life of the Prince Consort.*

Upon returning to the drawing room tea was taken while a selection of Welsh songs were sung on the lawn outside the French windows by twenty selected members of the Llangollen Choral Society, conducted by Mr. William 'Pencerdd' Williams. The Queen was much gratified, remarking to Lady Martin that she thought the voices more cultivated and better that any she had heard in Wales. She is said to have been 'visibly affected' when presented with a beautiful bouquet by Miss. Jennie Walker of 'The Willows', Llangollen.

Lady Martin died at their beloved Bryntysilio on 31st October 1898. Her body was conveyed to London for burial at Brompton Cemetery. There is a fine marble monument to her memory in Llantysilio Church. Sir Theodore followed her in 1909.

During the Second World War Bryntysilio was occupied by the military who, not surprisingly, left it not quite as found. About this time the fate of many large houses was in the balance. Restrictions still applied and it was also plainly obvious that the old way of life would never return. However, a Wrexham businessman, Mr. Sydney Aston, had both the courage and imagination to restore the house and gardens into the delightful home remembered by many, but found it necessary in so doing to reduce the house to about half its size. Eventually, Mr. Aston decided to retire to the Isle of Man. The property was purchased by a Walsall Educational Trust as an outdoor education centre and thus it remains today.

Plas yn Vivod lies across the valley from Bryntysilio and is the only Llangollen estate to survive with house and land more or less intact. The main house, built of local stone in the vernacular style, stands in its own delightfully secluded valley, on the site of an early farm house — probably called 'Meifod'. To this the present large edifice would bear no comparison.

Richard Ellerton, who as we know first lived at Bryntysilio, purchased the place before 1865, building upon the site the larger part of the mansion we see today. He later sold to William Wagstaff. Having taken a lease on Rhug near Corwen, Wagstaff was seeking a more permanent home for his family and one day chanced, by the merest accident of curiosity, to stray from the main road in order to see what was indicated by the sign 'Vivod'. Here they discovered Ellerton's property and were overjoyed upon discovering it to be for sale. A successful purchase was soon negotiated.

William Wagstaff, a solicitor by profession, was the son of Joseph Wagstaff (born 1791) of Westbourne House, Paddington, London. He not only extended the house at Vivod but also added further land to the estate. His only daughter, Mary, married Captain John Charles Best, RN of Abbots Anne, Hants, thereby establishing the dynasty of Best of Plas yn Vivod.

The present incumbent, Mr. Robert Best, is the fifth generation of his family to reside there. Of the last, Captain Harry Best, was a shy, retiring man much loved by his tenants and the town who steered the estate intact through many difficult days. He was a Justice of the Peace, a past Chairman of Llangollen International Musical Eisteddfod and an authority on antique clocks. Brother Frank was an expert on afforestation and arboriculture, while the surviving brother, Jack, is one of the famous Colditz escapees.

Plas yn Vivod was for many years home to the renowned Vale of Llangollen Sheepdog Trials, now removed to a new venue at Llandyn.

The Dinbren Hall estate is perhaps the most romantically situated of all, guarded as it is by both Castell Dinas Brân and the formidable Eglwyseg Rocks. Much visited by the Ladies of Llangollen, the Hall was built upon the site of an earlier house, part of which was incorporated into the present fabric until the house was reduced in size during the late 1950s.

One of the great joys of Dinbren was its wealth of trees. A fine avenue of yew stretched the distance of the long drive from lodge to forecourt. Another avenue of stately beeches ornamented the carriageway through the pleasure grounds. Seven splendid walnuts, known as the 'Apostles', graced the park. Sadly, the greater part of all of these were felled during the late 1960s.

Dinbren Hall and park in 1925.

Within the house is a suite of beautifully lit, large and lofty reception rooms which make up the south and east fronts of the main block. These were referred to in a letter dated 1795 written by a guest at Dinbren, Anna Seward (The Swan of Litchfield) to a Miss Wingfield:

"...four spacious rooms have been lately built and are yet unfinished."

The Dinbren House estate no longer exists as one holding, the various farms and properties having been sold off over the years, leaving the House and its few remaining acres isolated. Dinbren ceased to be a gentry house with the departure of the Scarlett-Smith family in the mid-1950s. Thereafter, it began its slow decline. Happily, Dinbren Hall has caring new owners and is being sympathetically restored.

The Tower, an ancient house first built as a look out for Castell Dinas Brân, stands below Dinbren. Its position allowed it to keep watch on a nearby fording place across the River Dee. Little visible remains of the original structure. W.T. Simpson reported in 1827:

"Some additions have been made to the Tower and it is now a comfortable farm house inhabited by a very respectable lady, of the name of Price. It has been a square building, built of hewn stone, as evinced by the massive walls which now surround the old part converted into a parlour, and by an old spiral stone stair at the back of the room."

The lady referred to would have been of the same family as John Price, FRS born at the Tower in 1734 and for forty-five years librarian at the Bodleian Library, Oxford. Later in the 9th century the house was, for a time, a private school. Two large rooms, set back from the main block on the south front, were built to house this. One is happy to report that the Tower remains a cherished house today.

Tyn Dwr Hall lies within the Pengwern Valley and has within its grounds what is considered to be the largest Yew tree in Wales.

The House is a Victorian erection in the 'Tudorbethan' style, featuring some black and white half timbering, stone mullions and a tower, all dating from c.1866–70. Inside, the impressive carvings are said to be the work of Bavarian craftsmen especially brought into the country for this purpose. Mr. John Dickin built the house upon land once

Tyn Dwr Hall in its parkland setting.

belonging to the old Pengwern Hall estate, who had various business interests within the area.

After his time the House had several further owners and tenants including a local millionaire, Hywel Hughes, who had made a prodigious fortune in Columbia, South America only to loose it in the Wall Street Crash. He was forced to sell Tyn Dwr almost before he had been able to enjoy it. Stoically, he went on to rebuild his empire and was worth an estimated three and a half million pounds at the time of his death in 1972. An example to us all!

A tenant for a while was Joe Duveen — later Lord Duveen (1869-1939) — who was probably the most successful antiques and picture dealer of all time. According to the lecturer and writer Robert Cumming, "Duveen extracted great masterpieces by guile, flattery and appeals to greed" having a "streak of ruthlessness, cunning, vulgarity, showmanship and charisma which is deplorable at a distance and irresistibly intoxicating when present in the flesh, eyeball to eyeball". What an indictment, but apparently well deserved. Duveen toured the country seeking out treasures, combing one defined area at a time, using as his base such houses as Tyn Dwr, before despatching the spoils to Duveen Brothers Galleries in London and New York.

For about forty years now, Tyn Dwr has been used as a youth hostel belonging to the Youth Hostel Association.

The Eisteddfodic Tradition

Put quite simply, the word *Eisteddfod* means a 'sitting together', but to many throughout the world it has come to mean 'Llangollen'. Few need to be reminded that this town gave birth to the first ever International Eisteddfod, but it is perhaps not quite so well known that it also cradled the Welsh National Eisteddfod, now such an important part of the cultural inheritance of Wales.

On the feast of the Epiphany in 1789 four bards, Jonathan Hughes and his son from Pengwern, Peter Lloydde of Cynwyd and David Jones of Rhos sat the long night through at the Hand, competing for a chair which had been made locally at a cost of ten shillings. The winner was Jonathon Hughes of Ty 'n y Pistyll, Pengwern, the house in which he had been born in 1721 and from which he was buried in Saint Collen's Churchyard in 1805, having spent all his life living and working on the little farm. Ty 'n y Pistyll still stands today, much altered and enlarged.

Ty 'n Pistyll — home of Johnathan Hughes — before its restoration.

Old sketch of the 1789 Bardic Chair.

George Borrow, when visiting Llangollen in 1854, chanced to call at the farm seeking directions, having determined to walk to Glyn Ceiriog. Here he met the grandson of Jonathan Hughes and upon quoting several lines written by the poet which, by incredible coincidence, he had read a mere thirty-two years before, was admitted with the words "Ah! I see you know his poetry. Come into the next room and I will show you his chair". This he described as "an antique three-cornered arm chair" and was further informed that Jonathan Hughes had also won a prize of fifteen guineas at a meeting of bards in London.

This same chair was for many years to be seen by visitors to Plas Newydd where it was placed on loan. However, we understand it to have been more recently removed by the owner, its present whereabouts unknown.

Eleanor Butler recorded in her journal on Monday, 5th May 1788:

> "Edward Evans of whom we enquired for his eldest son, a lad about fifteen, told us he had gone to London with a youth of his own age, son to Jonathan Hughes the famous Welsh Poet. They walked to Birmingham, then got on the Stage Coach, arrived in London on Monday."

The following year she recorded:

"... in soaking rain, Old Jonathan Hughes, the Bard of the Valley, with his poetical production at the Eisteddfod one of which he has translated. We sent for him into the Library: a tall venerable figure. Can speak very little English."

At this date he would have been sixty-seven, his 'poetical production' being that which had won him the famous chair.

Jonathan Hughes corresponded with bards in various parts of North Wales and with the Gwyneddigion Society in London in an attempt to raise support for an Eisteddfod to be held in Corwen, which in turn led to the Bala Eisteddfod, the first to which the public were invited.

In 1832 the Duchess of Kent, accompanied by her daughter the Princess Victoria, attended an Eisteddfod held at Beaumaris. They broke their journey by staying overnight at the King's Head, Llangollen, the inn thereafter changing its name to the *Royal Hotel.*

There were Chair Eisteddfodau in Llangollen in 1823, 1834 and 1831. Purely local ones also held in 1856 and 1857. There was much literary talent in Llangollen in those days, and there is little doubt that it was these *Eisteddfodau* which, in some measure prepared the way for the great Eisteddfod of 1858.

'Steddfod Fawr Llangollen', as it came to be known had, in modern parlance, very mixed reviews. It was also known as the 'Rainy Eisteddfod' because of the unceasing, intense downpours which caused Gwalchmai to pronounce "Broliwch yr ambrellas". The Eisteddfod was held on the Ponsonby bowling green and, as a result of lack of funding, only the most impermanent of structures could be provided. Hughes and Roberts, whose woollen mill stood close by, offered to supply enough good Welsh flannel to build a marquee seating 5,000 people in which to hold it. A generous offer, and splendid idea for the fine weather in which it was erected. Indeed, at first the construction looked, and stood, extremely well. Alas, as we know, the weather broke with a vengeance and the flannel proved to be woefully inadequate, stretching and sagging as the rains fell and the wind blew. Great pools of water gathered on the roof before cascading down onto the hapless audience. The ensuing chaos may be well imagined.

The 1858 Eisteddfod was indeed under-funded, for subscriptions had amounted to only £200. The Reverend John Williams (ab Ithel), one of the four major organisers, saw the reason for this to be strong and unreasonable prejudice against it. The higher classes, who could well have contributed much in financial terms, were against it because not one of them had been asked to preside. The Nonconformists were against it because the four leading lights were clergymen. The clergy in their turn were against it on a national basis, for fear that something might be said against the English Bishops in Wales. Curious indeed! Local organisers could not be found to serve on the Committee unless they were pre-indemnified against pecuniary risk! And the weather was most certainly against!

Thread-worn wax and thimble used to sew the 1858 tent.

Bearing all this in mind, the Eisteddfod was in many respects very successful and certainly of great importance. It was the progenitor of the National Eisteddfod in Wales. During the course of events, a Committee was set up to formulate a scheme for a central, permanent organisation. Much new and exciting talent was also brought to light from among the competitors, including Ceirog, Glasynys, Owain Alaw and Llwyfo.

The wonderful fresh voice of Edith Wynne charmed all who had heard it and she went on to become one of Wales's greatest vocalists. The late Mr. Charles Roberts of Ty Ddu, Llangollen who attended Eisteddfod Fawr as a young man of seventeen, often recalled the spine-tingling thrill with which he heard Llew Llwyfo sing the wonderful 'Glanrhondda', composed and written by a father and son collaboration. James James of Pontypridd composed the music and his father Evan wrote the words. Both of them must have been immensely gratified to see their composition adopted as the National Anthem of Wales. Charles Roberts, who died in his hundredth year in 1941, claimed never to have heard this so correctly sung as by Llwyfo.

The Eisteddfod also attracted an assortment of cranks and eccentrics, including the famous Doctor William Price of Llantrisant. His wild appearance — and curious habit of chanting pagan incantations to the moon wearing the unconventional garb of fox skin cap, mask and fur trimmed robes — must have caused a minor sensation. Doctor Price is now perhaps best known as the pioneer of cremation. Following the death of his favourite son for whom he had nurtured great hopes, he carried the body to a Llantrisant hilltop and destroyed it in a cast of burning paraffin. He died in 1893 at the age of ninety-three, having sired his last child — whom he christened Jesus Christ — at the age of ninety-one! A man of some stamina.

The Royal National Eisteddfod of Wales was held in Llangollen in 1908, the Gorsedd ceremonies having been held on the Hermitage Field adjacent to Plas Newydd into the grounds of which the stone circle was later removed. Here it graces the great lawn, to which it adds a touch of romance and mysticism. Once more, bad weather threatened to mar the occasion but decided to improve for the Thursday — the day upon which the famous David Lloyd George presided, surprisingly accompanied by Winston Churchill. The latter also addressed the audience, incorporating in his speech the only Welsh sentence he knew "Mor o gan yw Cymru I gyd" — "Wales is a sea of song". This had, of course, been taught him by Lloyd George.

This Eisteddfod was held on the (old) Vicarage Field opposite Fronhyfryd, in a specially constructed wooden pavilion, lighted by acetylene gas. Very modern!

The programme was conducted to a very high standard and it is interesting to note that the pianoforte solo competition was won by the highly commended Master Sydney Northcote of Bargoed, South Wales. The test piece was the first movement of Mozart's *Sonata in F*, no mean feat for a boy of ten years. Doctor Northcote, as he became, adjudicated at the first International Eisteddfod in 1947 and was a member of the Board for many years thereafter.

An outstanding and highly successful feature of the 1908 National Eisteddfod was the Arts and Crafts Exhibition held in the Council Schools, Parade Street, from 28th August to 10th September, opened by the Countess Grosvenor. There was a wonderful collection loaned from local people (Sir Watkin Williams Wynn, the Bangor University College, and so on) and there was also competitive work.

Esther Roberts demonstrated flannel weaving at her loom for the duration of the exhibition, the loom having being lent by Stephen Lloyd Jones of Dee Mills and reassembled within the school. Because of the inevitable noisy clatter of the process, this demonstration required a room to itself. The card setting machine was lent by Messrs. S. Harley

Esther Roberts at her loom. The costume she is wearing was made upon it by her brother Charlie and herself.

& Son of Clackheaton and the Petter Oil Engine by T. Charles Davies of Llangollen.

The other 'Special Demonstration' was of tooled leatherwork and hand lace making by Miss. J. Mercer of Oxford. Somehow, one fails to see the Welsh connection.

The Powys Provincial Chair Eisteddfod, a two day affair, was also held at Llangollen on the 3rd and 4th June 1932. The Gorsedd Ceremony was held at Plas Newydd on Saturday, 19th September 1931, the procession leaving Green Lodge garden at 2.30 p.m. Once again the Eisteddfod was held on the (old) Vicarage Field, under the presidency of Lord Howard de Walden.

Today, Llangollen is best known as the home of the International Musical Eisteddfod. It is so successful an annual event as to prevent, by default, the National Eisteddfod from ever being held here again. It would be quite impossible for the town to sustain two such major events within the same year, especially when one considers the vast amount of

organisation provided by unpaid volunteers.

From 1942–45 Mr. Harold Tudor, a journalist with a Liverpool newspaper, was released from his duties to assist the Northern Region of the British Council, an incorporated body, supported by Treasury grants, to set up and foster cultural relations between Britain and countries overseas. No mean feat during the war years. Mr. Tudor's particular brief was the care of distinguished allied and foreign visitors to National Eisteddfodau held at Bangor, Llandybie and Rhosllannerchrugog.

Several of these enquired of Harold Tudor if it would not be possible for groups from their own countries to take part in the choral competitions, a suggestion which he put to the Council of the National Eisteddfod. His idea was that an extra day or two might be added to the forthcoming 1947 Colwyn Bay Eisteddfod, but it was thought not to be feasible. Undaunted, the idea was then put to Mr. W.S. Gwynne Williams of Llangollen, music organiser to the Gorsedd of Bards, and to Mr. G.H. Northing, who had just been elected Chairman of Llangollen Urban District Council.

Mr. Northing, himself a talented musician, proved to be most enthusiastic and agreed to put the idea before his Council. They gave their support in principal and his next move was to invite some forty-two persons whom he considered would be interested to attend a meeting. This was held in the Council Chamber on 24th May 1946 in order to meet two members of the British Council — Mr. John Denison and Mr. Harold Tudor. The latter acted as liaison officer between the Council and Llangollen for the following fifteen months.

As a result, a scheme sub-Committee was set up which, at its first meeting the following June, invited Mr. Gwynn Williams to be Music Director and adopted the title of 'Llangollen International Musical Eisteddfod' for a proposed three day choral contest.

At a public meeting on 17th July the Eisteddfod was launched under the Chairmanship of Mr. Northing. But how to pay for it? There were no funds whatsoever for initial expenses, but within a short space of time £1,100 had been collected in the form of gifts, loans and guarantees. The Treasurer, Mr. E. E. Hughes, formulated a document promising to repay townspeople's loans in full if the 1947 Eisteddfod proved to be successful, or pro rata according to the takings.

The first Eisteddfod was held on the recreation ground above the town in a marquee — not sewn by hand or made of good Welsh flannel as had been the case in 1858. Llangollen, nor anywhere else for that matter, had seen anything like it. All available homes in town and the outer regions opened their doors to competitors and visitors alike. Overseas competitors were accommodated at no cost to themselves, but their journey to Llangollen was not without problems, including a French rail strike.

Altogether, forty overseas groups arrived representing fourteen different countries. The first of these was a Portuguese ladies' choir who had travelled 1,200 miles in their own motor coach, losing the way several times between London and Llangollen. And it rained! Hard and persistently for most of the time but somehow no one seemed to mind too much.

The opening ceremony took place at 6 p.m. on Wednesday 11th June 1947, followed by the evening concert given by Gwen Catley (soprano), Alexis Kligerman (solo piano), Robert Easton (bass) and Eleanor Dwyryd who sang to her own harp accompaniment. On the following evening the soloists were David Lloyd and Beti Gwynn Williams, whose fine contralto voice has been too rarely heard. However, seven years later during the afternoon of the Sunday prior to the 1952 International Eisteddfod, the BBC broadcast their regular *Country Magazine* programme from a temporary studio housed at the Grammar School. The soloist was Beti Gwynn Williams and the song *Llangollen Market*

The visit of Queen Elizabeth II and Prince Phillip in 1953.

had been arranged for voice and piano, especially for the occasion by her husband W.S. Gwynn Williams. As far as is known, this was the only occasion upon which it was sung in public in the town from which it was named.

It is a tribute to the success and popularity of the Eisteddfod that, by 1958, the original site had become too small for the event and some twenty-six acres of Penddol Farm land was purchased, together with the stone farm buildings, at a cost of about £7,500. And what an excellent site it has proved to be. Flat, with good road access and parking areas, picturesquely situated beneath the canal.

The idea of holding the proceedings in a large marquee had first been put forward by the late W.S. Gwynn Williams who had experienced their worth at first hand when adjudicating at the Anglesey Eisteddfod in June 1946. Rain, storm and tempest, which there were in plenty for that occasion, seemed to have little effect on the comfort of the audience or the quality of the acoustics, so the idea was adopted at Llangollen. However, as time went on the need for a more permanent building was keenly felt. There had been one or two difficult moments — especially in July 1974, when a fierce storm almost destroyed the marquee on the very eve of the Eisteddfod.

1992 saw the Festival being held for the first time in its own purpose-built, if perhaps controversial, building. In 1985 Lord Chalfont, a former president, had launched an appeal for the necessary £500,000. This, in days of great financial difficulties. However, after much hard work the target was achieved. Major contributors included the Foundation for Sports and the Arts, the former Glyndwr District Council, Laura Ashley Plc, Monsanto Plc, The Cefn Bryn Bequest, Lady Russon and the Margaret & Gwendoline Davies charities, as well as hundreds of smaller donations from individuals and well-wishers.

Her Majesty the Queen officially opened the Royal International Pavilion on 10th July 1992. It was not Her Majesty's first visit to the town. Accompanied by the Duke of

Edinburgh, Her Majesty first visited the Eisteddfod in 1953 very soon after her Coronation, arriving by train at Llangollen Station (which had been beautifully decorated for the event).

In 1964 her sister, the Princess Margaret, visited together with her then husband the Earl of Snowdon. Three years later, in the year of the Queen's Silver Jubilee, her daughter the Princess Anne made a popular visit in heat wave conditions.

Good weather also attended the visit of their Royal Highnesses the Prince and Princess of Wales in

Awaiting the Queen at Llangollen Station, 1953. What would Mr. Marwood have said?

1985 who, after what has now come to be known as a 'walk-about', joined the audience for the Tuesday evening concert.

And so the Eisteddfod continues to send out its special message to the world:

"Byd gwyn fydd byd a gano gwarriadd fydd ei gerddi fo."
T.Gwynn Jones

"Blessed is a world that sings, gentle are its songs."

There is much need for a great deal more singing in this far from gentle world.

The new Pavilion.

Lost Llangollen

Although Llangollen Fechan still exists (much-enlarged as a private nursing home), the large house on the hillside — extreme right — was destroyed by fire in the 1950s. Known as Bron Heulog, this was described by W.S. Simpson in 1827 as a recently erected mansion. "It is remarkable only for the narrowness of its windows and the nakedness of its appearance."

The Smith family standing in front of their general store on Regent Street. This they ran in conjunction with the Prince of Wales Inn next door. Behind, you can see the tall chimney of Cowards Timber Yard — now the site of Kwik Save.

Demolished in the late 1960s, this row of buildings in Hall Street stood where the car park now is. The three-storey gabled property was once a brewery and later the Ship Inn, while nailers lived and worked in the house with the anvil at second floor level (bottom left). The plaque was removed to the gable-end of the Willows.)

An unusual view of the rear of General Yorke's west wing at Plas Newydd (now demolished). The photograph below, taken at a later date, shows even more additions.

Arosfa Stables and a glimpse of the rear of the house. The long-time home of the Ffoulkes-Jones family, this house was demolished to make way for the Maesmawr Estate.

"Pen-Stepiau" cottages at the junction of Brook Street with Queen Street. Demolished to provide better access for the new fire station.

The demolition of Cemetary Cottages, Fron Bache. This pair of semi-detached dwellings were of pleasing appearance and enjoyed quiet neighbours.

Widening the road (1908) at the top of Hill Street. Hermitage House can be seen in the trees. Demolished for Local Authority housing.

Old shops in Church Street (note the paving of the road) and Roberts the Milk, Bryniau Bach, heading homeward at a much later date.

Demolition of the old Royal Oak Inn and Hand Hotel stables in the 1960s.

The field in which this cow happily stands is now buried beneath the Berwyn Road printing factory. The two white Ty 'n-y-Ffynnon cottages (extreme right) were demolished and the site developed.

Abbey Farm field still exists, but is buried beneath caravans.

Plas yn Pentre is happily still with us, but no longer looks as illustrated, its fine timbers have shed their stucco cladding.

The late Mr & Mrs Duncan Robertson at the site of old Llantysilio Hall.

Parson and squire! The Rev. Ivor Rees of Llangollen (1965–74) and the late Captain H.G. Best of Plas Yn Vivod.

Mr Laddie Jones of Bryn Melyn, with his beloved Mercedes sports car and Bob Owen, saddler, of Market Street, with a group of admirers.

The poacher who foolishly chose a Magistrate's estate and was caught not only by the keeper, but also the landowner's new camera!

Mr George Bradbury of Bryniau Mawr was a former policeman and friend to all.

Town characters Moses (Wilfred Jones) who claimed to have been born in the bulrushes and his companion, Taid Joss. In fine weather they invariably seized on a bench in the town centre from which they would offer unsolicited advice and comments to passing tourists.

A local WI production of a 'Pageant of Famous Women' (including the Ladies of Llangollen).

The Garner-Evans family, c.1915. Son Horace (left) qualified as a doctor and was sadly killed whilst on active service in the early years of World War II. Son Emlyn (right) became a barrister and was elected as an M.P. for Denbighshire (National Liberal) in 1951.

The late Emlyn Garner Evans, BA, MP, with his proud Mamma on the occasion of his first being elected for the Division. His mother kept a draper's shop at the top of Castle Street, now part of the Smithfield Inn.

Almost lost! Fire rages within the Town Hall a few days after Christmas 1964. It was found to have been caused by an electrical fault within the cold store wiring of the butcher's shop. Probably the strain of coping with too many turkeys!

Washing sheep in the hills above Llangollen, early 1900s.

Dipping sheep individually at Brynhyfryd Farm, Dinbren

Bob Owen, the saddler, greeting a customer c.1935.

Mr. J. Hiram Davies of Castle Street, County Councillor, Captain of the Fire Brigade and influential figure within the town. His standing can be judged by the grandeur of his funeral procession.

A horse-drawn pleasure boat on the Canal at Penddol.

Tourism

In March 1887 the Llangollen Council had an item on their agenda under the heading 'How to advertise Llangollen'. This seems to have caught most members largely unprepared, as very few positive suggestions were put forward. No one seemed certain as to whether or not the town should attempt to attract more industry, at the possible cost of making it less attractive to visitors, or indeed if a balance might be struck making it possible to accommodate both. It must be remembered that industry in those days normally meant noise, dirt and smell, presenting a pretty unattractive prospect.

A quick stroll about the town today leaves one in very little doubt as to the direction in which the pendulum has swung. A very large percentage of the shops could, perhaps unkindly, easily be grouped under the heading of 'tourist traps', selling phoney Welsh hats, dragon T-shirts, and any number of equally useless items suitable for taking back for Auntie Nellie who has been kind enough to care for cat or canary. There is Welsh marmalade, Welsh biscuits, Welsh toffee and an assortment of Welsh dolls, many with oriental eyes as a result of having being made in Hong Kong.

Were there ever so many eating places or restaurants? And still a goodly selection of Public Houses. 'Antique' shops sell anything from the real thing, to stripped pine (sometimes of doubtful vintage), to sneeze-inducing selections of dried flowers and pot-pouri. Newsagents offer a wide selection of magazines showing how to employ all these in giving one's suburban-semi the 'country look'. There is no doubt that tourism is now big business in Llangollen.

Today, the visitor is often only here for an hour or two and if staying overnight at one of the numerous bed and breakfast establishments, may well be doing so in order to rest

Looking across to 'Ham & Eggs Square'. Out of season, of course!

and refresh before moving on the following day. A hundred and more years ago, the picture was really quite different. Llangollen has had a stream of visitors ever since it became popular in the 18th century to admire romantic scenery. Amongst whom, of course, were the famous Ladies, Eleanor Butler and Sarah Ponsonby, who liked it so much they stayed here fifty years and attracted to their home at Plas Newydd notabilities too numerous to mention.

By the late 1800s visitors arriving by train were so great in number, especially at weekends when long excursion trains would arrive from Merseyside and the Midlands, that in 1897 the platform length had to be extended, as did the waiting room and other accommodation. A footbridge was also constructed, allowing passengers safer passage across the lines. Many of these would arrive hungry, having left home quite early in the morning and a favourite place of resort was Castle Street Square — famed for the substantial breakfasts served up in the front parlours of the cottages there, earning it the name 'Ham and Eggs Square'.

Horse-drawn (and later motor) omnibuses would be available in the Station Yard to convey those who were staying for a week or so — as many then did — to their hotel or lodging house. Others were ready to convey visitors to such beauty spots as the Horseshoe Falls and the Abbey. Excursions trains were of so great a length as to make it necessary to employ two engines, one at each end, in order to climb the Sun Bank gradient. The station staff was quite extensive and the Stationmaster was considered to be an important man. One such, Mr. Marwood, was well remembered by the late Mr. Carey Roberts, who as a young man had served under him. Mr. Marwood was a devout

A smart turnout in front of the Royal Hotel.

The arrival of a grand family at the Hand Hotel.

Christian but one who did not suffer fools gladly as Mr. Roberts remembered:

Lady Passenger:	"Mr. Stationmaster, can you tell me the time of the next train to Chester?"
Mr. Marwood:	"4.50, Madam."
Lady:	"Is there not one before that?"
Mr. Marwood:	"Not before the next, Madam."
Or, ...	
Passenger:	"Can you give me the time of a through train to Birmingham, Please?"
Mr. Marwood:	"12.16, Madam."
Passenger:	"And where do I change?"
Mr. Marwood:	"Change what?"
Passenger:	"I said, 'Where do I change?'"
Mr. Marwood:	"I think you asked for a through train, Madam."

Finally, ...	
Passenger:	"Can you give me an idea of the fare to Torquay?"
Mr. Marwood:	"Did you say 'idea'? Would you rather know the exact fare?"

All this in sharp contrast to a successor, the late Mr. Herbert Grainger, who was the most punctilious of mild-mannered men. He was so impeccably polite that he would even automatically raise his hat when speaking to a lady on the telephone!

Soon after the turn of the century, the *char-à-banc* was to become a common feature

Llangollen station staff, c.1895. Mr. Marwood is front row, centre.

Char-à-bancs parked in the Smithfield.

on the roads and they came in their numbers to Llangollen. A favourite means of transport for Bank Holiday and other organised outings, for which this town was a favoured place of resort, their arrival could well have heralded the beginnings of Llangollen's parking problems. They had to be left somewhere and so the Smithfield market place in the centre of town found a new use at times when it was not engaged in the auctioning of cattle and sheep. The photograph above gives some indication of the magnitude of the problem. One wonders who was in charge of the parking to have achieved such an

An interesting and early view of the Hand Hotel, now much altered.

orderly result and what might have happened should one of the middle vehicles have needed to leave early!

In order to feed all these people the enterprising saw a need for, and supplied, large capacity tearooms. The Glyn in Hall Street (once a tannery) was one of these and together with their other establishments, (all owned by Ivor Rowlands), the Corner Café, Castle Street and Gale's Café, Regent Street, boasted accommodation for four hundred people. Other establishments included the Waverley Tea Rooms — a large wooden building erected on land behind the Waverley Hotel in Regent Street. This hotel later became the local office of the Department of Health and Social Security (now departed), the tea rooms having been demolished. The Grapes Hotel built a long single-storeyed "parties catered for" dining room at the rear on the Regent Street side, complete with its own access. The Dorothy Cinema had a "quick service snack bar open 9 a.m. to 9 p.m." on the ground floor, and "Full service Café, Luncheons and Teas" on the floor above. At the rear in the large annexe was a special accommodation for "Party Catering a speciality. Menus and prices forwarded on request".

For the more discerning and those of means wishing to stay for a day or two as well as to eat, the two great competitors, the Hand and the Royal, both now elevated from Inn to Hotel, vied for patronage. *The Gossiping Guide to Wales* for 1896 has them glaring across at each other from facing pages.

"LLANGOLLEN"
EDWARDS'S HAND HOTEL
"THE HAND"
Unequalled for the beauty of its situation
On the banks of the Dee
Several
Bedrooms and Sitting Rooms
Have been added to the
House to suit the requirements of
FAMILIES VISITING THIS DELIGHTFUL NEIGHBOURHOOD
Table D'Hote, 7.00
Billiards
Omnibuses from this Hotel meet all trains at Llangollen Station.

And opposite:

SHAW'S
ROYAL HOTEL
James Shaw, several years with Mr. Mehl, at Queen's Hotel, Manchester, and from
County Hotel, Carlisle, begs to intimate that he has taken over the above
old-established Family and Commercial Hotel, and hopes by his thorough knowledge of the business, to merit the patronage of visitors to this lovely vale.
The Hotel is close to the far-famed Llangollen Bridge and overlooks
the River Dee.
Coffee Room, with unequalled view. Ladies' Drawing Room, Private Sitting
Rooms, Large and Airy Bedrooms, and all the comforts of a home. Table D'Hote
at separate tables.
Billiard Room
Tariff on application to
James S. Shaw, *Proprietor.*

The Royal Hotel before extensions. Note the building (extreme right) now a branch of HSBC, then occupied by the Post Office.

Regardless of Mr. Shaw's extra outlay on typesetting, it would seem that the Hand just about won that particular round on points — at least for the time being. Soon afterwards producing a rather impressive little booklet sub-titled "A Souvenir of the Hotel with the Proprietor's compliments". And who do we find that proprietor to be? None other than the verbose Mr. James S. Shaw, formally of the Royal Hotel!

By now the Hotel was able to boast sixty bedrooms, some with large private sitting rooms. The splendid little brochure illustrates an amazingly cluttered entrance hall with grand staircase, together with excellent photographs (all by J. Percy Clarke of Llangollen) of the writing room, billiard room, banqueting room, coffee room, drawing and dining rooms as well as a view of the commodious private sitting room. Much emphasis is also placed on the new-found 'pleasures of motoring' and contains several exciting photographs of vehicles of the day, as well as a less exciting view of "The Hand Hotel Motor Garage. Accommodation for 30 cars. Posting in all its branches. Separate lock-up for six cars". On another page is a photograph of General Roberts leaving Llangollen by open car after, one is certain, an enjoyable stay at the Hand Hotel. The reader is also given "A Handy List of distances by road from the Hand Hotel" and a whole page and a half is devoted to "Motor Index marks for the United Kingdom", Denbighshire being 'CA'.

After all this, being so freely given, who could possibly stay elsewhere? But many did and there was much choice. Smaller licensed or 'Temperance' hotels abounded through-out the town and there were numerous guesthouses and persons simply letting rooms. There was a choice of 'Full Board' or 'Keep Yourself' where by the good landlady would cook and serve such food as was provided by her guests.

The usual thing was for families to stay for a week or longer — the dream of so many

B&B proprietors today. Children were not allowed to become so easily bored and much encouragement was given to use their legs as well as eyes and ears, learning to appreciate the simple joys of the countryside. Fishing nets were sold in town and could be used for chasing butterflies, or even fishing when the young hopeful would march determinedly river-wards, armed with bamboo-poled net and a jam jar swinging from improvised string handle (usually provided by some kind-hearted landlady). Anything to get the little 'luvs' out of the house!

In order to 'cash in' on the rapidly expanding visitor boom, one or two large houses were built with a view to providing the extra bedrooms required. Two of these were 'Springbank' at the top of Birch Hill and 'Ashgrove', strategically placed at the corner of Berwyn Street and Market Street. The latter was convenient for the town, river and pleasure gardens, while Springbank was not for the faint- (or weak-) hearted, boasting fine views from most bedrooms if one survived the ascent from town!

Later, the fashion for cycling and development of the gear-change 'racing' models, made it possible for the less well-off, and others given to the pleasures of healthy exercise, to travel away from home at little cost. Llangollen became accessible for a day-trip from such places as Merseyside and the Midlands. 'Cyclists Welcome' notices appeared outside many of the smaller establishments and indeed welcomes were being extended everywhere. 'The Welcome Board Residence' in Bridge Street advertised their 'Reasonable terms, homely and central' accommodation with the jingle:

"We Welcome All
Who come this way
To 'The Welcome'
For to stay.

Well they tried! The exception was perhaps the 'Cheerio Guest House', Regent Street, which seemed anxious to say goodbye before one had arrived. Perhaps their much-promoted 'modern spring-interior beds' made up for it. Here they also had cellars, claimed to be "beautifully dry" and fitted with bunks for cyclists.

Children today would probably find Llangollen very dull after a day or so due, mercifully, to its lack of instant entertainment. There are neither fun fairs nor amusement arcades. Once, there were two coin-operated slot machines, positioned outside Gracie's Castle Street Emporium. One took a penny, where-upon a glass-cased gypsy queen, wearing a veil would apparently write out one's fortune, pen automatically moving from side to side in stiff-wristed hand. Upon completion, a printed card would appear from a slot in the base, neatly proclaiming ones fortune. A second penny would produce quite a different prophecy, and so on until the seventh coin was inserted, when fortune number one would re-appear and so the cycle continued.

The other machine cost only one halfpenny but was not so glamorous. Instead, the palm of the hand was placed on a brass plate in order to have it read. Upon insertion of the coin, a number of small studs set into the plate moved up and down until one's palm had been well and truly read. Then the card would appear, following roughly the same procedure as the more expensive variation. All good fun, but now no longer possible as both machines disappeared some forty years ago!

As we have seen, the years have brought many changes within this remarkable little town, with the certainty of many more to come. But the river will run and the surrounding hills continue to protectively shelter the huddle of houses we call Llangollen.

Perhaps the future tourist may, like the modern hiker, simply stay the night and pass on. Like Hazlitt, having enjoyed the view from the Holyhead Road after leaving Froncysyllte:

"It was an April day and the valley glittered green with sunny showers, like an amphitheatre, broad barren hills rising in majestic slate on either side with green upland swells that echo to the bleat of flocks below and the River Dee babbling over its stony bed in the midst of them."

Like him, no doubt, other travellers will say, "I would return sometime or other to this enchanted spot". As so many have returned, if only in their thoughts.

Let the last word go to the *British Weekly*, which in 1893, stated:

"Llangollen is a beautiful place and can never be dull unless to very unreasonable people!"

To which we add a last *Amen*.

Ashgrove, Berwyn Street. Purpose-built for tourists. (Photo: J.A. Pedder-Roberts)

View of Cerrig y Llan c.1860 showing the newly-built St. Johns Welsh Church (middle left).

L'Envoi

And so this book has come to its conclusion. But the story has not ended for Llangollen. In common with all other towns, Llangollen continues the making of its history on a daily basis. Limitations of space dictate that much has been left out, but it is hoped that what remains is enough to persuade the reader that they have not wasted time.

My thanks are due to Mr. Ron Thomson for his willing help with photographs and to Mrs. Peter Walker for kindly allowing the use of several from the family's collection. Also to the Lady Trevor and the late Professor Barri Jones for so generously providing aerial views. Special thanks are due to Mr. Roger Mansbridge for typing and so valiantly translating my handwriting into legible English. Let us hope it has all been worthwhile.

Gordon Sherratt,
Fron House, Nr. Llangollen.

Bibliography

Thomas Pennant	*A Tour in Wales*
Lord Mostyn and T.A. Glenn	*History of the Family Of Mostyn of Mostyn*
W.T. Simpson	*Some Account of Llangollen And Its Vicinity*
George Borrow	*Wild Wales*
Fletcher Moss	*Pilgrimages to Old Houses*
A.G. Bradley	*The Romance of Wales*
Mrs. G.H. Bell	*The Hamwood Papers of The Ladies of Llangollen*
	The Dictionary of National Biography
	Transactions of the Denbighshire Historical Society — Various years
	Llangollen Advertiser — Various Years
E. Ellis Hughes	*Eminent Men of Denbighshire*

Bridge, tower and weir, c.1930.

Index